ROLLS-ROYCE

75 YEARS OF MOTORING
EXCELLENCE

Foreword by
Lord Montagu of Beaulieu

ROLLS-ROYCE

75 YEARS OF MOTORING EXCELLENCE

Edward Eves

CRESCENT BOOKS · New York

First English edition published in 1979 by Orbis Publishing Ltd

This 1982 edition is published by Crescent Books, distributed by Crown Publishers, Inc.

h g f e d c b a

Printed in Czechoslovakia

Library of Congress Cataloging in Publication Data

Eves, Edward.
    Rolls-Royce: 75 years of motoring excellence.

    Bibliography: p.
    Includes index.
    1. Rolls-Royce automobile. I. Title.
(TL215.R6E93 1982)   629.2'222   81-19628
ISBN 0-517-37485-4   AACR2

This book was created by
Eldorado Books Limited, London

Design: Mike Strickland
Picture research: Sam Elder, Anne Horton, Nicky Wright

Special photography: Nicky Wright

Special thanks to Mel Petersen

Above: Twenty drop head coupe by Compton on a 1926 chassis
Endpapers: 40/50 Ghost about 1910 with Barker body (National Motor Museum)
Half-title page: 1925 Twenty coupe by Barker (Nicky Wright)
Frontispiece: The Silver Ghost and a Camargue (Rolls-Royce Motors)
Pages 6-7: 1925 Silver Ghost tourer by Barker

CONTENTS

FOREWORD
by
Lord Montagu of Beaulieu

What is the mystique of Rolls-Royce? That it exists is apparent from the freezing silence that greets foreigners proclaiming the rival virtues of Cadillac or Mercedes-Benz, and from the wave of shock and gloom that attended 1971's financial *debacle*. It was almost as if a well-loved monarch hovered between life and death.

Certainly, it does not stem from advanced engineering. The original 40/50 of 1906 may have been more refined than its competitors, but its design was conventional for the period. Handwork may distinguish a modern Royce from other cars, but before 1914 mass-production methods were hardly understood outside America, and even then the Name's primacy was recognized.

If we talk of styling, we have a somewhat stronger case: after all, that splendidly Grecian radiator has withstood many an onslaught, including one from Royce, who regarded it as too complicated and expensive to make! But it is also fair to point out that before 1949 no Rolls-Royce as such wore a factory-built body.

So what is the answer? First and foremost, we may seek it in Henry Royce's own ideas. Perhaps fortunately, his near-fatal illness exiled him physically from Derby and so prevented him from carrying them to what would be (for him) their logical conclusion. He remained, however, a perfectionist rather than an innovator. He took the best *proven* ideas and developed them to the point of absolute reliability. Other cars might be faster than a Rolls-Royce; they might be more accelerative, more sophisticated, easier to drive and cheaper to repair. One might even dare suggest that some, when new, could rival its silence. The difference was that after double the average automobile's lifetime, a Ghost or Phantom would still be delivering new-car performance to new-car standards. The last Ghosts of 1925 might be antiquated from a technician's viewpoint, but for an owner content with silence, 65mph and the ultimate in top-gear motoring, they were as good as any new model.

Hence, throughout the 1930s, we find many an aged Royce being updated – four-wheel brakes on the real ancients, wellbase wheels, new radiators, skirted wings and the latest in body-styles.

Nobody wanted to ride around in a perpendicular box, but why waste a chassis still in the prime of life?

Nor was this the end of the road. Other Royces were passed on to the garage and funeral trades, to serve as wreckers or hearses, while between 1939 and 1945 the survivors earned their keep in Civil Defence. Typical of these faithful servants is my own Phantom I, supplied new as a tourer to my father in 1925. It spent the war as a mobile canteen in Bath and ended 30 years of hard work hauling a gang-mower round a village playing-field in Somerset.

There is another factor that is often forgotten: the one-model policy pursued from 1907 to 1922. Charles Rolls disapproved, and it was a perilous course to pursue in those days of multiple

ranges. But it paid off. During the formative years, a Rolls-Royce was by definition a luxury six of over seven litres' capacity. There were no Tens and Twelves for the middle-classes. There were no taxis, either; if you flagged down a cab in London in 1912 it could well have been a Napier, recognizable by the 'water tower' on its radiator.

Daimler catered for almost everyone save the true marginal motorist. Of the foreigners, there were 11 Mercedes models and nearly as many variants of Delaunay-Belleville. More heads of state, it is true, still chose the French and German giants, but this was not the point. It is surely significant that by 1920 Isotta Fraschini, Lanchester and Napier were all down to one model, and that a luxury type. Delaunay-Belleville, who stayed with a wider range, were destined for a long, slow and painful decline.

And the mystique lives on. In this book Edward Eves has sought to present the marque 'warts and all'. He has examined the breed's opposition at every stage of the saga. Some readers with experience of these, from the double-six Daimler to the twin-cam Duesenberg, may question the validity of the mystique. But how many of them can base their views on 250,000 miles at the wheel of the same car? And how many of the breeds which have challenged, or are currently challenging, Rolls-Royce have the same background of 75 years of continuity?

Montagu of Beaulieu

The Hon Charles Stewart Rolls
(1877–1910), sculpted by Lady
Scott. This statue, erected at
Dover, commemorates Rolls's
cross-Channel flight of 1910

Sir Frederick Henry Royce
(1863–1933) by Derwent Wood,
RA, at Derby. Royce, a
commanding figure over 6ft tall,
was created a baronet in 1930

CHAPTER 1

The Men behind the Marque

Britain in 1860 was a very different country from the one we know today. The railways had recently begun to spread their net across the countryside. The stage coach and the carrier's cart, travelling on waterbound roads, remained important elements in the nation's transport system. Victoria's Prince Consort was still alive, the Whigs were in power, public hangings could still be witnessed. But change was coming. The Great Exhibition of 1851 had proclaimed Britain's industrial might and inspired the nation to further progress in practically every field but road transport. There had been attempts at running steam coaches but vested interests in horse transport halted further developments. It was left to Etienne Lenoir in Paris in the early 1860s to start the ball of automobilism rolling when he made a 7-mile jaunt from Paris to Joinville-le-Pont in a lash-up carriage powered by a gas engine.

Even in the tiny village of Alwalton, some 5 miles south-west of Peterborough, things were changing. James Royce, scion of a long line of millers from South Luffenham, 12 miles away, was busy converting his flour and bone mills to steam power. His wife, Mary, a farmer's daughter, was preparing to present him with their fifth child. Apart from the mechanical instincts it may have inherited no-one could have predicted the influence this child would have on the whole area of mechanical transport. The baby was born on 27 March 1863 and four months later was christened Frederick Henry Royce.

James Royce's attempts to mechanize his mills ended in financial failure in 1867 and, disheartened, he took his family off to London. Hardship followed for some years and the children contributed to the family finances in whatever way they could. Young Fred, as he was known then, sold newspapers for W. H. Smith and Sons at Clapham Junction and Bishopsgate and his mother took a job as a housekeeper. In these straitened circumstances schooling took second place to the need to live, but things improved sufficiently to enable him to attend school from the age of 11 to 12. Then it was work again, this time as a telegraph messenger at the post office in Mayfair.

At this stage an aunt in Fletton took pity on the boy and paid for an apprenticeship at the new Great Northern Railway works in Peterborough. The cost was £20 a year. She also paid for his keep with the Yarrow family. Frederick was doubly fortunate, for he found his work instructive and absorbing and Yarrow himself was a skilled fitter and machinist with his own lathe, shaper and tools in a back-garden workshop. What Royce did not learn at the railway works he was taught by his landlord. His skill with machine tools was probably learnt in the garden shed.

In 1879 Royce had his apprenticeship cut short when his aunt, affected by the slump, could no longer afford to support him. It was not the best time for a 16-year-old to find work but Royce was not easily put off. Most of the engineering works were in the north of England so there he went, trudging up the Great North Road to Bradford and Leeds carrying testimonials from the superintendent of the locomotive works which, as Yarrow's son wrote later, 'should have got him work anywhere'. In Leeds he eventually found employment with a firm of toolmakers at a salary of 11 shillings for a 54-hour week. What little spare time he had was spent studying the new science of electrical engineering that was to become a lifelong passion.

He was confident of his knowledge of electricity and when a job was advertised as tester with the Light and Power Company in London he applied for the post, and got it. Street lighting by electricity was in its infancy but Royce's mechanical ability, allied to his knowledge of the subject, not only proved adequate but caused him to be sent north as technical adviser to the newly formed Lancashire Maxim and Western Electric Company in Liverpool. When the parent company in London folded the Lancashire company also closed but the episode had lasted sufficiently long for Royce to have acquired valuable experience and knowledge. When he was not working he attended lectures at the London Polytechnic and became a protege of Professor Ayrton, the battery pioneer. Moreover, he had accumulated a little capital.

The ups and downs he and his family had experienced imbued him with the determination to succeed. To this end he formed a small manufacturing company in Manchester with a friend and fellow electrical engineer, Ernest A. Claremont. His stake was £20 and Claremont's £50. The first jobs in their workshop in Cooke Street were subcontracts for lamp parts and small switchgear. As motive power for their machinery they used a steam engine that Royce had been given by a friend. The partners lived above the workshop and prospered modestly through hard work, prudence and Royce's intense concern for detail and his mechanical and electrical expertise. Experience with generators at the Light and Power Company had given him an understanding of electric motors. He realized that mechanical ability as well as electrical knowledge was essential in that field.

In 1893 Royce and Claremont married the daughters of Alfred Punt. They also acquired the services of John De Looze, who would look after the financial side of the enterprise, then booming because of the electric motor business. No doubt it was on the advice of De Looze that F. H. Royce and Company was reconstituted as a limited company in 1894 when the manufacture of cranes began. It was now known as Royce Limited. The directors were Royce, Claremont (who proved a talented businessman), a friend of Claremont and De Looze. As secretary and accountant De Looze subjected every item of expenditure to searching scrutiny.

Although they were his bread and butter Royce knew all about the shortcomings of DC motors and generators and was an early enthusiast for three-phase current for workshop use. The drum-wound motors the partners produced as their capital grew were eagerly taken up by the textile trade and by mine owners for hauling gear. Then came the first Royce workshop cranes, driven by his motors, which were a complete innovation. They not only made money but took the pulley-hauley out of a lot of factory jobs that had hitherto called for lifting tackle and muscle power. The impression has often been given that the cranes were small equipment and that the undertaking was a minor one. By the turn of the century many of these products were, in fact, travelling cranes for dockside and steel mill use propelled by motors of up to 70hp rating, with sophisticated switchgear, all built and designed by the company, which was soon able to maintain a considerable drawing office, steelworks and foundry all under the supervision of Henry Royce. The cranes were a big success because they were well made, quiet running and extremely long lived. They were also expensive. Royce's precept was always that the quality remains when the price is forgotten. In times of financial stability this is not a bad principle, but it tends to be forgotten when there is a heavy drain on finances, for example in a recession. It worked well enough in the golden 1890s to the extent that the company's capital was increased to £30,000 in 1899, equivalent at today's values of almost £1 million.

Before he even thought of motor cars, therefore, Royce had become a man of substance, a respected mechanical and electrical engineer. Success did not change his habits to any extent. True, he developed a liking for gardening at his home in Knutsford, doing it at night by the light of an electric bulb on the end of a garden cane stuck in the ground, but in the works he remained a dynamic combination of designer, chief inspector, critic, and father-confessor to his 'boys'. Yet somehow nothing that was done was ever really good enough. His standards were invariably exacting.

The turn of the century was a difficult time for the British economy. The slump that followed the Boer War affected all aspects of business. The position was made worse for Royce Limited by price cutting indulged in by newcomers to the crane

Ernest A. Claremont, Royce's original business partner, was the first chairman of Rolls-Royce. On his house was a crest and the legend 'Be industrious'

business attracted by the Manchester company's success. That Royce became interested in motor cars in this period appears to have been a coincidence and at first he did not consider them as an alternative product to cranes but simply as an efficient means of transport. The De Dion quadricycle, his first purchase, could hardly have been so described, yet this crude but ingenious device may well have triggered in him the desire to make something better. It is certainly behind the remarks he made later in life about the crudity and general mechanical inferiority of early motor cars. His approach to the problem of improvement set a pattern that he followed in later years. It was to go out and buy the best example of what he wanted, take it apart and then build a better one. It was a straightforward approach that served him well.

Once Royce had made up his mind to make his own car his partners well knew that they could not gainsay the project. His opinion was formidable and his determination impressive. Moreover, he had been right in the past so they stood back and allowed precious resources and manpower to be diverted into building a batch of three cars. Two apprentices, Eric Platford and Tom S. Haldenby, helped erect them. Royce, a hard taskmaster, inspired intense respect and loyalty and both Platford and Haldenby stayed with him until their retirement. Platford became chief tester when Rolls-Royce Limited was founded in 1906 and ran the final test department in the 1920s. Haldenby was a right-hand man to Royce when he planned the Derby factory and was in charge of buildings and maintenance there. He was later instrumental in laying out the factory at Crewe.

The interior of the Cooke Street factory, Manchester, in 1904. By then Royce's engineering business had been established 20 years

It was not by chance that Henry Edmunds entered the picture. A company director by profession and a keen motorist and amateur driver by inclination he first became involved with Royce Limited when Claremont approached him to buy a block of shares in the cable-making firm of W. T. Glover of Salford, of which he was a director. As a pioneer electrical engineer – he introduced the incandescent lamp to England – he knew Royce well. Edmunds lived in London and commuted to Manchester regularly. Moreover, as a member of the tightly knit motoring community he was friendly with Lord Llangattock's son, the Hon Charles S. Rolls. From conversations with Rolls he knew that his firm of C. S. Rolls and Company, which sold quality French cars, was anxious to market a really high-quality British motor car. Royce was busy making two-cylinder vehicles, while

Rolls preferred three or four cylinders, yet Edmunds knew that Royce's car was as refined and well built as anything in his experience and that Rolls would approve. Royce refused to go to London to meet Rolls, so Edmunds persuaded Rolls to make the journey to Manchester. The men met over lunch at the Midland Hotel in May 1904. Afterwards they tried the car. Rolls was captivated by the vehicle and by the man. No mean mechanic and a qualified engineer himself, he undoubtedly saw that, while the Royce car was better than good, the man who made it, given the right encouragement, had the talent to build infinitely better machines. He returned to London proclaiming that he had found the best motor engineer in the world and sent Claude Johnson, his partner, to assess the car and make business arrangements.

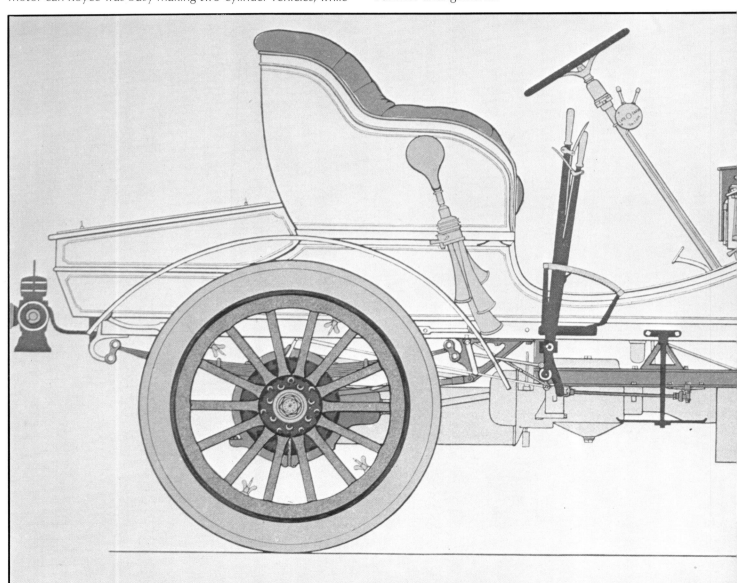

Charles Stewart Rolls was a pioneer of motoring in the United Kingdom. As a young man of 19 studying engineering at Cambridge he had imported a 3½hp Peugeot of the Paris-Bordeaux type and shattered the tranquility of the university town. In common with the Hon Evelyn Ellis he had used his car freely on the public highways, disregarding the 4mph speed limit and the requirement to be preceded by a man with a red flag. Only the wealthy could afford motor cars at that time and it was their influence, and that of the Self Propelled Traffic Association that they formed, which caused the speed limit to be raised to 12mph in November 1896.

In his way Rolls was as dedicated a man as Royce. Having espoused motoring he did it impulsively when and where he could, always with the emphasis on competition. He won, for example, the 1,000 Mile Tour organized by the Automobile Club of Great Britain and Ireland. With the Hon John Scott-Montagu he shared the honour of being the first Briton to race abroad. That was in 1899 when he competed in the Paris-Boulogne race driving a 12hp Panhard. He finished last by a considerable margin and realized he had much to learn. The following year he rode as mechanic to S. F. Edge in the 1900 Paris-Toulouse-Paris event on a 16hp Napier, the first-ever British car to challenge the continentals on their own ground. He drove his own 60hp Mors in the historic Paris-Berlin race in 1901 but failed to reach Bordeaux in the 1903 Paris-Madrid. Subsequent to meeting Royce, he drove a Herbert Austin designed 96hp Wolseley in the Gordon Bennett race of 1905. His eighth position in the big international race of the season was an outstanding effort.

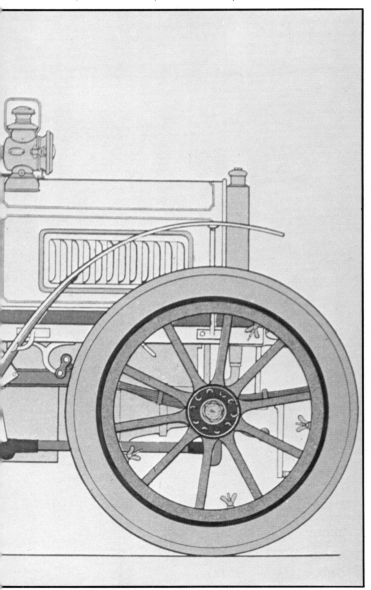

Left: The 1904 10hp two-cylinder Rolls-Royce had an engine capacity of 1,800cc. The complete car cost about £400

Above: Charles Rolls, as drawn by Spy. Rolls specialized in selling top-quality cars to a distinguished list of clients

Rolls had set up in business in London as an importer and vendor of high-class French cars early in 1902 and traded from Lillie Hall in Seagrave Road, Fulham. As with most things he did the enterprise was well organized. A feature of Lillie Hall was an extensive machine shop, equipped to make spare parts that could not be obtained from the manufacturers, and space to display used cars. A showroom in Brook Street in the West End was opened later prior to the final move to Conduit Street in 1905. The cars he supplied to a noble clientele were mainly Krebs-Panhard, Mors, Minerva and Clement. The discovery of Royce and his car pleased him enormously because he was an intense patriot and was irked by the refusal of British designers to learn from the advances being made by their counterparts in Europe. So Rolls and Johnson undertook to sell all of Royce's car production. The agreement signed in 1904 provided for Royce Limited to make cars for a new firm, Rolls-Royce Distributing Limited; the cars would be known as Rolls-Royce.

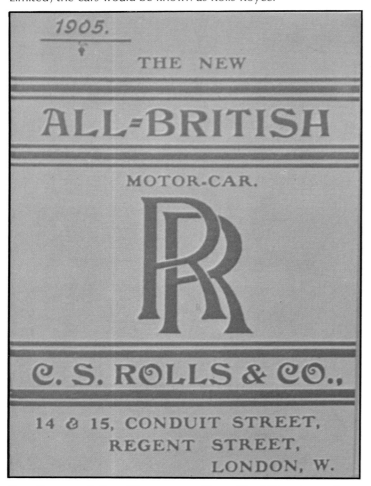

Almost two years elapsed before the partners decided that the time was ripe to form a full association and for Rolls and Johnson to concentrate their energies on selling Rolls-Royce cars exclusively. Rolls-Royce Limited was registered in March 1906 with a nominal capital of £60,000. The new company took over all the assets of Rolls's company and the car activity of Royce Limited, which continued to make cranes. Claremont and Johnson, meanwhile, looked for new premises for the factory and Royce busied himself with designing a successor to the 30hp six-cylinder car.

That a new factory and a new model called for more capital became apparent when the design of Royce's new 40/50hp crystallized and the cost of building and equipping the new factory was assessed. The 40/50 made a triumphant debut at the Olympia motor show in November, the month the decision was made to increase the capital of the company to £200,000 and offer half the shares to the public. This was not easy. As Johnson pointed out, Rolls was a popular figure but not substantial enough for the City, Royce was virtually unknown and he, Johnson, was merely a mediocre businessman. History was to reassess that last statement. To give the share issue added authority two people were approached. Paris Singer, a well-known businessman, owned the first production 10hp Rolls-Royce car while A. H. Briggs, a wealthy woollen manufacturer from Bradford, was already a shareholder and an enthusiast for the vehicles. Singer was not prepared to help but Briggs supported the issue and when it looked like failing he wrote a cheque for £10,000.

To separate car manufacture from Cooke Street, where the crane business was brisk, a number of sites were examined. One of them was alongside the Cooke Street premises, off Stretford Road. Others were at Bradford and Coventry. Then Derby Corporation offered a substantial tract of land at Osmaston.

Preceding page: Rolls and the 96hp Wolseley that he drove to eighth place in the Gordon Bennett Cup of 1905

Above: The 1905 catalogue of Rolls and Co announced the Rolls-Royce range. This is the cover of a facsimile reprint

Top: Rolls acquired Lillie Hall, Fulham, in 1902 as a repair shop and garage. It had once been a roller-skating rink

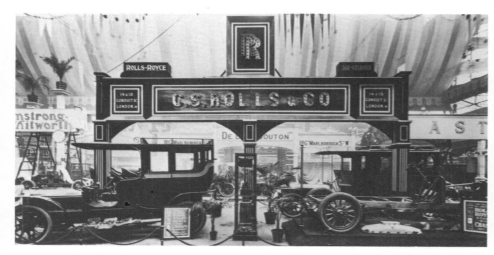

Claude Goodman Johnson has been described as the hyphen in Rolls-Royce; he was certainly a remarkable man. A couple of generations back his ancestry seems to have been little different from that of Royce. He described his forebears as 'tradesmen, farmers and yeomen'. Johnson's father failed as a tradesman and moved to more amenable employment in the science and art department of the South Kensington museum where he rose to the position of curator. He was a devoted father and did night duty at Bethnal Green museum to pay for his son's education at St Paul's School and South Kensington Art School. Claude soon discovered that he was not cut out to be an artist and he found employment at the Imperial Institute where, as part of his duty to arrange shows and exhibitions, he helped organize the Great International Motor Exhibition promoted by Harry J. Lawson's Motor Car Club in 1896. The exhibits assembled from many manufacturers brought home to a distinguished gathering the significance of self-propelled personal transport. Furthermore, the part that Johnson played in mounting the exhibition did not go unnoticed.

When Lawson's Motor Car Club was revealed to be a body designed to promote his trading activities many pioneer motorists moved over to the newly formed and independent Automobile Club of Great Britain and Ireland, founded by F. R. Simms and Harrington Moore in 1897. With recollections of the Imperial Institute exhibition, Simms and Moore invited Johnson to become secretary. In this job, where he was often called upon to organize competitive events, he inevitably came into regular contact with Rolls. The friendship was confirmed when Rolls convincingly won the gold medal in the club's 1,000 Mile Tour on 23 April 1900 driving a 12hp Panhard. At a dinner held later Johnson was presented with £100 to mark the club's appreciation of his work in the race. The award was proposed by the Hon C. S. Rolls.

The Rolls stand at the 1906 motor show at Olympia, London. The chassis of the new 40/50 model is on the right; on the left is a 30hp six-cylinder limousine

Top: Claude Goodman Johnson (1864–1926) understood the value of publicity. He worked tirelessly to promote Rolls-Royces in trials and races

Above: The 15hp three-cylinder was one of four models first made by Royce for Rolls to sell from his London showrooms. It was produced in 1905

It was not surprising, therefore, that when Rolls started his business he should ask Johnson to join him as a partner. Johnson had become disappointed by the development of politics within the automobile club and was happy to run the new business while his partner got on with his motor racing, ballooning and flying. These activities not only brought Rolls excitement, they also provided publicity for the firm and attracted many clients.

Given his flair for running trials and demonstrations it was natural that Johnson should have sought to demonstrate Rolls-Royce cars by these means. He thought up the 15,000 mile trial for the 40/50 Silver Ghost, the London-Edinburgh run and suggested participation in the Alpine Trials. On another level his wisdom was never more apparent than in 1911 when he persuaded Royce, seriously ill from overwork and dietary neglect, to quit the factory and live in semi-retirement with a personal drawing office nearby where he could supervise engineering designs. This separation from the factory meant that Royce had to learn to commit his design thoughts to paper as well as verbally to the stream of designers shuttling between the works and his retreat. The effect of this was to create a body of engineers who worked and thought like Royce. Furthermore, by persuading the board to adopt a one model policy from 1906 to 1922 with the 40/50, Johnson helped secure the company's financial security and its reputation for quality products.

Johnson was responsible for establishing a winter home for his engineer-in-chief at the little village of Canadel-sur-Mer, near Lavandou on the French Riviera. A convinced Francophile, Johnson had built his own Villa Jaune there two years before Royce's health collapsed. After a convalescence at Overstrand in Norfolk where a nurse, Ethel Aubin, looked after him, Royce was taken to the Villa Jaune further to recuperate and to get him away from the factory. The spot enthralled him so much that Johnson bought a plot of land next to his and had a villa and attendant buildings constructed in 1912–13. Royce became a semi-invalid and his wife, Minnie, parted company with him. It cannot have been a very satisfying marriage for her. It was a childless one and she saw little of her husband because of his preoccupation with work. From then on Royce was nurtured and cared for by the ever-present Aubin, whose attention and encouragement extended his life by many years.

1908 ROLLS-ROYCE 40/50

Even before Royce separated himself from the works the company suffered a severe but not disruptive loss with the death of Rolls. Long before he had met Royce, Rolls had been fascinated with flying those globular, lighter than air machines, balloons. He was Britain's foremost aviator, was a founder member of the Royal Aero Club and was on the point of trying to establish, against his partners' wishes, a Rolls-Royce aeroplane company. For some time he had ceased to be involved in the actual running of the motor car company. He was a great friend of the brothers Eustace, Horace and Oswald Short who built his balloons. After Wilbur and Orville Wright demonstrated heavier than air flight, the Short brothers built Rolls a Wright Flyer under licence. In this machine, in June 1910, Rolls became the first Englishman to fly the Channel and since he did not land on the other side but turned over Sangatte and flew back, he became the first man to make a double crossing nonstop.

For the Bournemouth flying meeting a month later on 11 July the Shorts had modified the Wright by adding a tailplane according to designs issued by the French constructional company. The work was carried out to the letter although Rolls's head mechanic had reservations about the design. Despite gusty conditions the second day of the meeting featured a landing competition. Of the three machines that preceded Rolls's flight two were damaged on descent. Then it was Rolls's turn. His approach was steep, over the grandstands. He found himself undershooting, and at about 20ft he pulled back the controls to lift the nose of the Wright. Suddenly there was the crackle of breaking wood, the superimposed tail boom crumpled and the machine nose-dived into the ground. Rolls was killed instantly by concussion.

Left: This drawing of a 1908 40/50 Ghost shows the Roi-des-Belges style by Barker. More than 7,800 were built of this, the most famous of all Rolls-Royce models

Top left: Royce, Ethel Aubin and their dog relax in the sun
Top right: This photograph of Rolls appeared soon after his Channel flight of 2 June 1910

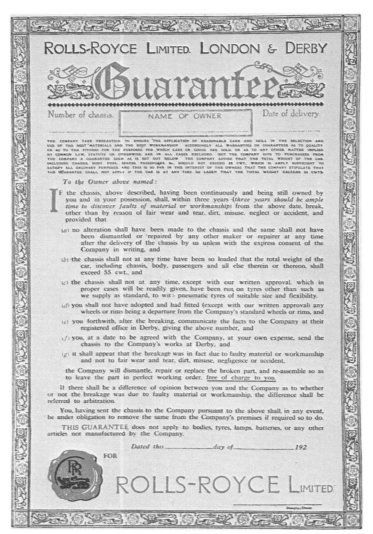

ROLLS-ROYCE LIMITED. LONDON & DERBY

Guarantee

Number of chassis.   NAME OF OWNER   Date of delivery

*This three-year guarantee against
chassis defects was reproduced
in a 1921 catalogue*

into metal and give it to the experimental department to have it rig-tested, road-tested and redesigned until it was perfect. If he had a shortcoming it was that he tended to waste time on refining the design of components before he had finalized the overall design. The Rolls-Royce 'Bible', a carefully pruned collection of memos between Royce and the Derby design team and experimental department, reveal his insistence on the finest obtainable finish for working surfaces and the best materials.

From before the First World War Royce's British home had been at St Margaret's Bay, Kent; later he shifted to a house and farm at West Wittering, Sussex, away from the bombs. The drawing office at West Wittering was located in the village about a mile from the house.

In 1919 Royce's design team was headed by T. S. Barrington; A. G. Elliott and Bernard Day answered to him and R. C. Hall looked after metallurgy. In the 1920s Elliott was Royce's chief aide at West Wittering and Le Canadel. Day was chief of the drawing office and Charles Jenner chief engine draughtsman. Day oversaw chassis design and Ivan Evernden correlated the work of the chassis engineers and the coachbuilding companies that bodied the chassis. At Derby, initially, E. Harvey Baillie and Maurice Olley were chief production draughtsmen until Olley went to the United States to launch the Springfield project. Ernest W. Hives, assisted by W. A. Robotham, was chief experimental engineer.

While Royce exerted absolute authority in motor car design the aero-engine side, which had started in 1914, he left to Elliott and A. J. Rowledge in the 1920s. Royce, however, dictated policy and was ready to intervene if he saw things going the wrong way. Arthur Sidgreaves took over as general manager from Basil Johnson who had assumed the duties of chief executive upon the death of his brother in 1926. Sidgreaves, under the chairmanship of Lord Herbert Scott, guided the company through the difficult, yet busy, prewar period and for most of the war years before he died in 1944. It was in these years that the aero-engine side expanded greatly.

Royce's exile from the works — and that was effectively Cooke Street, for his visits to Derby were very rare — called for a considerable duplication of design effort and a cumbersome method of working, but Claremont and Johnson knew well that Henry Royce was the firm's biggest asset. The arrangement adopted in principle was that Royce should have, near his house, a drawing office with a resident team of designers-draughtsmen who would turn his ideas into working drawings. In common with many great designers Royce was not a draughtsman and conveyed his ideas in notes and sketches. The drawings from his 'bureau' were sent to Derby where the parts were made up in the experimental department and tested. Royce believed that the only effective way to judge a product was to get something

Ostensibly the weakest link physically in the chain, Henry Royce survived all his original partners. After his death in 1933 the outstanding figure to emerge was Ernest Hives. As chief experimental engineer he had been responsible for making Royce's designs work. He made parts from drawings sent from Royce and put them on the road to be broken or proved. He had joined the company in 1908 as a tester cum competition driver, he drove a 40/50 Ghost in the 1911 London-Edinburgh run and was a member of the works team in the 1913 Austrian Alpine Trial. In the 1920s, when Royce tended to be over-preoccupied with detail, Hives made many important engineering decisions and offered them for judgment to his chief engineer. As often as not he would drive the cars down to Le Canadel

himself, sometimes in company with Robotham, who later became chief engineer.

Hives could be both exasperating and inspiring. He disliked delegating authority and seldom gave praise. But his decisions were sound and sometimes inspired, such as when he decided that the only engine for the Rolls-Bentley 1931 was the 20/25hp unit suitably hotted up. He is said to have had a sixth sense as a driver. There are many tales of how he would cut blind corner after blind corner and then suddenly take the correct line on the next one – when there was invariably a car coming the other way.

He made his mark as generalissimo of the aero-engine programme working under Rowledge and Elliott, although the whole episode was very much a Derby operation. In 1936, on the retirement of Arthur Wormald through ill health, he was appointed general manager of the works and was largely responsible for getting the vital Merlin production scheme under way. Impatient with civil service bickering Hives persuaded the board to build what was the best light-alloy factory in Europe. It was to prove of enormous importance in the conduct of the war for without it Britain could well have lacked Merlin engines in quantity in 1939. Another far-sighted, Johnsonian move he made was to swap Meteor tank engine production for the Whittle gas-turbine project, which had been given to the Rover company but was proving a little beyond them. In so doing he laid the foundation for the modern-day aero-engine business.

Between Royce's death and his own retirement Hives brought along men such as Robotham, Dr Llewellyn Smith and Harry Grylls to carry on the Royce tradition of design and workmanship. Hives and Elliott became joint managing directors in 1945 and Hives went on to become the first engineer to be appointed chairman of the company. T. S. Haldenby, who had helped build the first Royce car, succeeded him as general manager. Royces, as the firm was known in Derby, rarely let a good man go. And they made many a good man that much better.

Top: In 1914 Rolls-Royce issued a French catalogue that contained these two colour photos by Percy Northey, a company salesman and driver. A phaeton torpedo 40/50 is on the left, a limousine landaulet on the right

Above: Ernest, later Lord, Hives started as an apprentice with Charles Rolls and became chairman of Rolls-Royce. This photo shows him leaving Buckingham Palace in 1943 after his investiture as a Companion of Honour

Above: The back entrance to the Cooke Street premises. In the part at the end of the alley the first Rolls-Royce cars were built in 1904

Opposite: The second car built by Royce went to his partner, Ernest Claremont. The 10hp two-cylinder is shown here outside the Cooke Street office

CHAPTER 2

Cars from Cooke Street

Henry Royce's purchase of a 10hp Decauville of approximately 1902 vintage had been preceded by his decision to buy a De Dion quadricycle, which he bought as a more efficient means of personal transport than a bicycle or pony and trap. Although it may have been a fast and effective machine for its time the quadricycle offended his engineering instincts. His choice of a Decauville, however, was a sound one. It was well engineered and had a record of reliability. A 5hp model had completed a 1,000 mile nonstop run at the Crystal Palace cycle track and a 10hp car had made a nonstop return trip from London to Edinburgh.

The Decauville 10hp was of what we now consider conventional layout. At that time automotive designers were still debating whether the engine should be at the front and whether the drive from it should be to the back axle via a countershaft and chains or gearing in the axle. Renault had put a live axle into production in 1901 and had mounted it on semi-elliptic springs. He had used a torque stay to absorb the braking and driving loads. The Decauville incorporated a front engine, Hotchkiss drive and an all-enclosed gearbox, features that undoubtedly conditioned Royce's choice. It was a very useful machine, but one Royce knew he could better.

By the time of its maiden run the first Royce car embodied all these design features. Royce had clearly decided to make his own version of the French car and to correct the design faults against which all his instincts as an engineer rebelled. Moreover, he constructed the machine to much higher standards of workmanship and materials. Both cars had two-cylinder engines of approximately the same capacity. The French one had bore and stroke of $4\frac{1}{3}$in × $4\frac{1}{3}$in (2,090cc) while the British one featured dimensions of $3\frac{3}{4}$in × 5in (1,800cc). In common with the French car the Royce engine had a cast-iron cylinder block mounted on an aluminium crankcase.

But there the similarity ended. In line with the latest developments in Europe, the inlet valves of the Royce were positively opened by push-rods, operated by an extra camshaft, instead of being of the atmospheric type that were sucked open against the action of a light spring by the downward movement of the piston on the induction stroke. This latter method was common practice on small cars. The camshafts were operated by gears enclosed in a dust-proof timing case at a period when on even the lordly Mercedes they were open to the air – and dust and mud.

Royce fully appreciated that it paid to take the mixture from the carburettor to the inlet valves along the shortest possible route. His induction manifold was of generous cross-section and of almost modern appearance compared with others. By cunning modifications he had also persuaded a French Longuemare carburettor to respond far more readily to the wishes of the driver than its makers had ever intended or achieved. On the third of the first batch of three Royce cars he fitted a carburettor of his own manufacture based on that designed for Panhard by Commandant Krebs. This particular carburettor gave instant and controllable engine response, a rarity in those times, although it was still under the control of a centrifugal governor operating a valve in the induction pipe. Manual override was provided. Royce had made his own high-tension, trembler-coil ignition system with a distributor incorporating built-in governor. But he relied on a French-made Carpentier coil to provide the spark.

In one fundamental aspect the engine differed from some other twins of the period. At that time the normal practice was to use a single-throw crankshaft for twin-cylinder engines with the pistons rising and falling together. Taking advantage of the four-stroke principle the pistons fired on alternate strokes, thereby giving an even firing note. Royce saw the disadvantages of this system, which caused the engine to vibrate like a large single-cylinder unit even if balance weights were applied to the crankshaft. He realized that a two-throw crankshaft, with one piston going up when the other was going down, would give much better mechanical and dynamic balance although the firing impulses would be uneven. He knew that dynamic balance was more important to the smooth running of the engine than

The first Royce chassis is shown without its fan. The complete car (inset, beside a 40/50 Ghost) was used as a company runabout

the uneven but relatively weak firing impulses. This point of engine design was more fundamental to the smooth running of the first Royce car than any other. Further to insulate the occupants from vibration Royce mounted the engine and gearbox in an underslung subframe.

He hushed the 'hop-and-carry one' exhaust note endemic to the layout by fitting a monumental silencer. (A modern parallel of the two types of engine is seen in the Triumph twin-cylinder motorcycle engine, which has the pistons coming up together, and the Honda equivalent which has them raised alternately like those of the original Royce car.)

Many of the chassis and transmission details of the Royce car were also inspired by the Decauville but there was closer attention to detail. The back axle, for example, was of the Decauville type with fully floating half-shafts, which entailed mounting the wheels on bearings on the outside of the axle trumpets. All this work was carefully carried out with large,

well-proportioned bearings that were quite at variance with French practice. Another feature, which persisted in Royce-designed cars for many years, was the provision of a steady-bearing for the nose of the final-drive bevel pinion. It was an early indication of Royce's appreciation that metal is a flexible engineering material. By providing this extra support the final-drive gears were made much quieter. The only drawback was that a spur-wheel differential had to be used to make room for the steady-bearing housing.

A leather-faced internal cone-clutch transmitted the drive from the engine to the sliding pinion gearbox, in which the gears were selected by a quadrant lever with a neutral between each gear. Aluminium was used wherever possible including for the gearbox casing, the clutch housing and the lower half of the engine. The result was that the finished vehicle weighed $14\frac{1}{2}$cwt against the Decauville's $16\frac{1}{2}$cwt. It was one of the lightest cars in the four-seat, 10hp tourer class. The engine was rated to give 10hp on the brake at 1,000rpm but 12bhp was more likely.

U44, the oldest surviving Rolls-Royce, dates from late 1904. The body of this 10hp two-cylinder was extensively modified and the car allowed to deteriorate before it was rescued and restored to original condition in the 1950s

Top: Claremont's 1904 Royce car was later sold to W. T. Anderson, who is shown at the wheel
Centre: AX148, a 10hp Rolls-Royce with 1905 body
Above: U44, built in 1904 and still running well

This first car was no lash-up. Admittedly the frame did not have pressed side-members but was constructed from commercial steel channel with forged front and rear dumb-irons, yet it was complete and finished in every detail. And even at this early stage all the bolts used to hold fittings to the chassis had taper shape; Royce had little time for rivets. The specification seemed unlikely to set the world on fire but the car's performance and its manner of going was quite out of the ordinary. It had its first run on 1 April 1904 from the Cooke Street factory to Royce's home at Knutsford, 13 miles away. Fitted with temporary test body, it was driven by Royce and followed at a respectful distance by Eric Platford in the Decauville. The journey was without incident. When two more cars were completed they went to Ernest Claremont and Henry Edmunds. Claremont's car was not entirely trouble free. Claremont himself was no mechanical genius and to avoid the inevitable embarrassment in the event of a breakdown he fixed a brass plate to the dash which read: 'If the car breaks down don't ask a lot of silly questions.' He later acquired a four-cylinder 20hp machine and the Royce car was sold to the contracts manager of W. T. Glover and Company. After a number of years it was donated to a technical college in Manchester.

The secret of the Royce car was undoubtedly its engineer's flair for design. All the parts were beautifully proportioned, carefully fitted and provided with adequate means of lubrication. Royce had learnt much about gear tooth forms in the course of building cranes, in which the gears were particularly quiet. Manchester was then a world centre for the manufacture of textile machinery and what the Manchester machinists did not know about gear-cutting was hardly worth knowing. Every gear on Royce's cars, including the timing gears, was enclosed and running in oil. The oil was distributed to the engine and transmission via a set of drip feeds from a cast aluminium tank mounted on the dash and pressurized by the exhaust system.

After agreeing in 1904 to supply vehicles for Rolls to sell, the little Cooke Street workshop had to work feverishly to produce the promised samples of 15hp, 20hp and 30hp Rolls-Royce models for exhibition at the Paris Salon in December of the same year. A complete 10hp and 20hp were backed up by a specially finished 10hp show chassis, there was a 15hp standard chassis without engine and a 30hp six-cylinder engine.

Despite the urgency involved, the two-cylinder 10hp engine put on show was practically a complete redesign. Typically, Royce was not satisfied with his original 10hp and time was found to give the twin-cylinder car a new, three-bearing crankshaft with each throw operating in its own chamber in the crankcase. This arrangement prevented the oil from swilling to the back of the sump on hill-climbs and was an important factor when big ends depended on splash lubrication. Special attention was paid to lubrication because Royce had considerable problems when test-running his original engine. An oil pump, driven by a spring belt off the end of the camshaft, drew oil from a 1 gallon tank located underneath the crank chambers and pumped it to four sight feeds on the dashboards whence it was distributed to the engine bearings, clutch and gearbox. Inside the engine the oil was picked up by big-end dippers from shaped troughs in the bottom of the crankcase, thrown around the engine, found its way to the main bearings via collecting rings and was then returned to the main reservoir.

On these cars the entire ignition system with the exception of the batteries was designed by Royce and made at Cooke Street. It utilized a Royce double-trembler induction coil and a distributor mounted on the end of the crankshaft. This was not the high-tension ignition system we know today but one that relied on a coil in which the high-tension pulses were induced by a vibrator, rather like that on an electric bell, instead of by an engine-driven contact breaker. The high-tension current was doled out by a simple wipe-contact commutator and on each stroke the plug of these slow-running engines got not one but many sparks on each firing stroke.

A feature of the Paris Salon cars was the standardization of engine parts, which was really the reason the cars were ready in time. All except the three-cylinder engine had cylinder bores of $3\frac{3}{4}$in and a crankshaft stroke of 5in. The cylinder blocks were cast in units of two cylinders. Thus the four-cylinder engine simply had two cylinder blocks and the six-cylinder engine three. All engines had the same design of crankcase with the main bearing caps cast integral with the base castings that incorporated the oil troughs. All of them had the same oil pump supply to sight glasses and the supplementary hand pump feed to the main bearings for starting and high speed. A refined version of Royce's own Krebs-based carburettor was used and had the then-usual centrifugal governor with override by the accelerator. The three-cylinder engine had three separate single-cylinder blocks and a crankshaft with the throws set at 120 degrees. This engine also had 4in bores but in other essentials it was the same as the other models. Later on the bore size of the 10hp was increased to 4in.

As far as the chassis was concerned the 10hp Rolls-Royce car retained the built-up chassis with straight side-members and forged dumb-irons featured on the Royce 10hp. The larger models had pressed steel chassis of differing sizes in keeping with the engine power. The 10hp, for example, had a 75in wheelbase but the 15hp had a wheelbase of 103in and on the 30hp it was $116\frac{1}{2}$in. Later in the production of the 20hp cars a heavy 20hp model was introduced with a 114in wheelbase to take a limousine body. A long-wheelbase 30hp measuring 118in was also offered.

While the twin-cylinder and three-cylinder cars featured

semi-elliptic springs on all four corners, the heavy 20hp and the 30hp cars had what has been called platform rear suspension. In this layout the rear ends of the rear springs were shackled to the ends of a transverse semi-elliptic spring mounted in the middle of the rear cross-member. It has been suggested that mounting the axles of the 20hp and 30hp cars behind the centre line of the side springs imparted a degree of roll resistance at the back. Even if this had been so the effect would have been nullified by the action of the transverse rear spring which would have had the effect of reducing the rear roll resistance and must have caused considerable understeer.

Top: SD661 is a 15hp three-cylinder of 1905 owned by the Royal Scottish Automobile Club
Above: Colonel Ruston poses in his 1905 two-cylinder

V.C.C.
1905
ROLLS-
ROYCE
4

SD-661

Above: When not participating in
veteran rallies SD661, the only
known survivor of the 15hp
model, is housed in the Doune
Motor Museum in Scotland

Overleaf: This 30hp six-cylinder
is the sole survivor of its type.
It was rebuilt from a rusting
chassis and some parts that were
rediscovered in the 1950s

It is difficult to be categorical about all the transmission arrangements of the Rolls-Royce cars shown at Paris in December 1904. Certainly the rear axles were of the Decauville full-floating type. Production versions of the 20hp and 30hp models were offered with four-speed gearboxes having direct drive on third gear and what was effectively an overdrive top that was later christened the 'sprinting gear'. Production 30hp cars had ball-bearing hubs on all wheels. A notable feature on all these cars was the internal expanding rear wheel brakes, operated by the hand brake in the manner of the times. They were well designed and proportioned with provision for internal adjustment from one shoe to the other and adjustable brake stops to prevent rattle. A transmission brake working off the foot pedal was also provided.

Six-cylinder cars were just coming into vogue, accompanied by a great deal of controversy, and received much publicity mainly through the efforts of S. F. Edge of Napiers. Rolls, who specialized in powerful cars for the nobility and gentry, believed a six-cylinder was essential for his range. At the time the crankshaft arrangement for six-in-line engines was far from established and Royce's first 30hp six featured a six-throw crankshaft carried on seven main bearings with each pair of cylinders treated as if they were a 10hp twin and each pair of throws arranged at 120 degrees. Thus the balance of the engine, irrespective of power impulses, was that of a three-cylinder which had quite strong primary and secondary rocking forces however good the static balance of the shaft and pistons.

Of the pre-1907 cars the 20hp was undoubtedly the pick of the bunch for the discerning driver. The 10hp was really just a refined runabout; the three-cylinder was the odd one out and had vibratory problems which caused it soon to be dropped. For the sporting motorist, the 30hp six-cylinder, though luxurious, was just too cumbersome. But the 20hp in its original form had the essential ingredients of a good power-to-weight ratio, excellent weight distribution and a smooth-running, willing engine that gave more than its nominal horsepower at its rated 1,000rpm and could be taken faster if need be. It was the ideal vehicle with which to promulgate the new and relatively unknown marque.

British participation in motor racing had got off to a slow start. Initially the British had viewed French enthusiasm for this noisy, oily pastime with a mixture of contempt and indifference, although a few of the more farsighted drivers such as Charles Jarrott, Rolls, Cecil Bianchi, S. F. Edge and others had seen its value in furthering the development of the motor car. Attitudes changed when Edge won the 1902 Gordon Bennett race, which had been run as part of the Paris-Vienna event. The rules now required the 1903 Gordon Bennett to be organized by the national automobile club and for the race to be held in the United Kingdom – where any kind of motor racing on the king's

highways was expressly banned, although in all probability the sporting Edward VII would not have minded one bit. If the race was to be held in the British Isles something had to be done – and it was, by a group of Irish MPs who pushed through a Bill permitting the event to be staged in Ireland.

The following year when it came to holding the eliminating trials to choose the British team for the 1904 Gordon Bennett, the governor of the Isle of Man, Lord Raglan, was quick off the mark in suggesting that the island would make a splendid venue. Inevitably the next move was for a British motor race – and what better place for it than the Isle of Man?

Thus the Tourist Trophy was born. Motor racing in Europe was clearly in decline as a result of the minimum weight rule that encouraged monstrous racing freaks bearing no resemblance to the kind of cars people wanted to buy. The automobile club's Tourist Trophy race, announced in late 1904, would by contrast be run to a set of rules designed to encourage a healthy type of high-speed touring car. Briefly, the rules required a chassis weight between 1,300lb and 1,600lb carrying a load of 950lb, of which 250lb had to comprise the body and 700lb the driver and mechanic and a suitable load of ballast representing passengers. The amount of fuel that could be carried was limited to $9\frac{1}{4}$ gallons. The cars had to do four laps of a 52-mile circuit right round the island, taking in Douglas, Castletown and Peel, as well as a number of railway level crossings.

The 20hp Rolls-Royce was ideal for the event. A. H. Briggs, an enthusiastic director, saw to it that Charles Rolls was one of the first to enter. Two cars, both lightened by a nickel-steel chassis frame and axles, were carefully prepared in Manchester for Rolls and an amateur, Percy Northey. Another special feature of the cars was the already-mentioned overdrive top gear; direct drive, on third, was ideal for mountain-climbing. Rolls's car had a big bore, 4in engine.

Claude Johnson behind the wheel of a 30hp six-cylinder prior to a public trial against a four-cylinder Martini in 1906. The Rolls-Royce emerged the winner

Above: Percy Northey leads Rolls in the 1905 Tourist Trophy, a drawing by F. Gordon Crosby. Northey took second place but Rolls broke down

Top: This 20hp TT production replica was built from the parts of two identical chassis. The body is a copy of the 1905 TT car
Above: The car's ignition and throttle controls are in the centre of the steering wheel

Held in September 1905, the race was a cliff-hanger to the last minute. Rolls broke his gearbox when, after coasting down from the start to Quarter Bridge in neutral, he attempted to engage gear at too high a speed and stripped the teeth on third and top. Northey, left to fly the flag, responded with a fine drive and crossed the line first, but John S. Napier in the opposed-piston Arrol-Johnston took less time from the staggered start.

Northey's second place provided a tremendous boost for the marque. Claude Johnson lost no time in publicizing the result and kept the 20hp in the public eye throughout the winter. A TT Replica was added to the range of cars and demonstrations of its low-speed, top-gear performance were given in the Mall, London. The public were also shown how the car could climb Jasper Road, Sydenham, a 1-in-6 gradient, in top gear with nine people on board. These demonstrations showed that the vehicle could comply with new regulations for the 1906 TT.

A further demonstration of the all-round ability of the 20hp was given in May 1906 when Rolls and Northey took two cars, a 1905 TT Replica 20hp and a prototype of the 1906 TT car, down to Monaco with the aim of assessing their relative merits and measuring fuel consumption. On the return journey they planned to celebrate the anniversary of the Monte Carlo-London 'record', set the previous May by Charles Jarrott in a 40hp Crossley, by beating the time. The Crossley's average speed had been 24.2mph. Despite bad weather and Rolls's refusal to turn back when he took wrong turnings, the 20hp, four up, averaged 27.3mph to Boulogne and was then forced to wait for more than three hours for the next boat. Rolls just managed to scrape into London and beat Jarrott's time by 1½ minutes. Jarrott complained that, unlike Rolls, he had not had his eye on the clock but he got his revenge a year later when he knocked more than 2 hours off Rolls's time for the journey.

Massac Buist, Rolls's navigator, later recounted how, on the way out, he noticed that the provisions included two bottles of champagne and a copious supply of cold tea. When this was remarked upon Rolls explained that the champagne was for him and the cold tea was for the others. And at organized stops Rolls would dash into a hotel to change while the rest of the party refuelled and changed wheels.

Henry Royce's second essay at car design at Cooke Street is generally reckoned to be his least auspicious. It may have been a failure commercially but the design was excellent. The vehicle was a petrol brougham with the maximum speed regulated to the legal limit of 20mph. Lord Northcliffe had gone into print with his belief that the era of open cars and 'speed mania' were things of the past. He suggested further that the ideal all-round

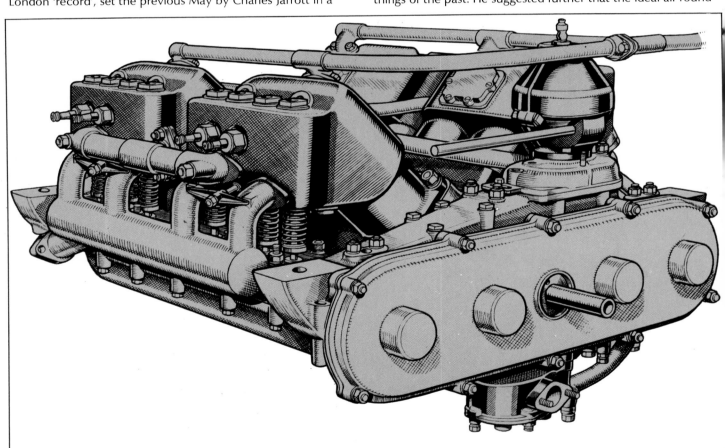

vehicle would be a petrol-driven equivalent of the electric brougham, which had a strong following because of its 'noiselessness and the absence of vibration and smell'. The noble lord went on to say that the sporting carriage no longer had any attraction for many motorists who simply desired a comfortable, modest-looking vehicle with sufficient power to maintain 20mph.

Whether or not these words persuaded Johnson to commission the design, or whether Northcliffe actually ordered such a car, Royce's design was masterly. The engine especially marked a significant step forward and incorporated many features that were carried over into the superb 40/50 a year later. The main problem involved hiding the engine in what was primarily a bonnetless car, although a version with a bonnet was also planned. Royce's answer was to design a side-valve vee-8 with the cylinders set at 90 degrees, and with a shallow sump, which could be tucked away alongside the driver. The only indication of its presence was a slightly higher floor in the engine area.

Engines with the cylinders arranged in a vee were not novel in 1905 but they were few. Daimler's first twin-cylinder engine had the cylinders arranged in a narrow vee and Levavasseur had built an impressive vee-16 for his graceful Antoinette monoplane. But Royce's decision to use eight cylinders set at 90 degrees was innovatory and set a pattern for compactness that has since become universal in the United States. Having achieved a compact layout in cross-section – the engine was rather long – he next tackled the problem of smoke, almost always found with splash-lubricated engines. He gave the engine a fully pressure-fed crank supplied by a gear pump driven by worm gears off the nose of the crankshaft and picking up oil from the aluminium sump in the modern manner.

The single-plane crankshaft had hollow journals and crankpins, closed by small dished plates, and was fed with lubricant via drillings in the main journals. A notable advantage of this arrangement, which was carried over to the 40/50, was that each hollow crankpin acted as a tiny oil reservoir. A further advance was that separate main-bearing caps were used for the first time in a Royce engine instead of incorporating them in the lower crankcase casting.

The use of side-valves in line was also new to Royce and marked a step forward from the early overhead inlets which were really only mechanically operated atmospheric valves and were left in the head by habit rather than with the object of improving combustion. The layout of the valves, arranged vertically and therefore at 45 degrees to the cylinder axes, allowed Royce to interpose a long idler lever between the cams and the valve stems. It also gave a more direct flow of mixture into the head compared with the conventional layout.

Cylinder dimensions of this unique engine were $3\frac{1}{4}$in × $3\frac{1}{4}$in –

Opposite: The eight-cylinder engine built for the Legalimit

an indication of things to come – giving a capacity of 3,535cc. The cylinders, water jackets and heads were cast in pairs. In the absence of exact details of the engine internals it has to be assumed that the three-bearing crankshaft had an inordinately long centre main bearing because there was a not inconsiderable gap between the two blocks forming each bank. Through it the long induction pipes passed from the single Royce carburettor. However, the location of the plugs on the wrong side of the inlet valves from the combustion chamber, and alongside them, can hardly have helped combustion.

The choice of a single-plane crankshaft, which is prone to create small secondary shaking forces in the engine but gives equally spaced power impulses, was a nice choice if Henry Royce was aware of it. Quite recently with the Coventry-Climax racing engine Walter Hassan turned from the two-plane to the single-plane crankshaft in the interests of improved exhaust characteristics and found the out-of-balance forces quite tolerable and far less than had been expected. Reports on the performance of the one and only Invisible Engine in a 'Landaulet par Excellence', delivered to Lord Northcliffe, effused on the smoothness and lack of gearchanging, confirming the correctness of the design.

The alternative Legalimit model with the engine in the proper place covered by a long, low bonnet was exhibited in two-seater form in 1906. But there were few takers for a $3\frac{1}{2}$-litre car with a maximum speed of 20mph – it would do very little more – and the model was dropped after three cars had been built. Yet it proved to be a useful exercise in design and many lessons were learnt in anticipation of Royce's greatest engineering achievement, the 40/50hp side-valve engine.

A sketch of the bonnetless eight-cylinder landaulet of 1906

In September 1905 the *Autocar* sampled the first 15hp to be completed, for a Mr Hodson of Liverpool, and in the same month *Automotor Journal* reported on a top-gear run from Salisbury to London in one of the 30hp six-cylinder cars. A more tangible demonstration of the 30hp came when Johnson accepted a challenge from Captain H. H. P. Deasy, later to be associated with the Siddeley-Deasy car, to match the 30/40hp four-cylinder Martini which he was then importing with any six-cylinder. Johnson saw to it that the test, which included entry in the 671-mile Scottish Reliability Trial and then final assessment for quietness and smooth-running (by a panel of stockbrokers), received adequate press coverage. The Rolls-Royce won by a good margin due, in part, to a derangement of the Martini's fuel system.

Johnson's flair for publicity amounted to genius. For the Tourist Trophy races in the Isle of Man a 30hp Rolls-Royce was at the disposal of officials as a matter of course. The 1906 race was run over a shortened circuit of 162 miles to eliminate most of the railway crossings of the 1905 event. Rolls and Northey went over to the island two months in advance to learn the circuit and accurately set the carburation, for again a fuel limit was imposed that would require the cars to average 25mpg. New rules increased the minimum wheelbase to 96in and required the cars to traverse the promenade in Douglas in top gear at 12mph. Both Rolls-Royce cars had 4in bore engines, liberally drilled chassis frames and a set of Rudge-Whitworth wire wheels that Rolls reckoned would be worth 30 seconds a lap and were definitely quicker to change in the event of tyre mishap. Just as significant was the direct drive third gear, which gave best efficiency where it was most needed – on long climbs.

Fortunately for Rolls the Arrol-Johnston was plagued with tyre troubles although Napier's speed on the first lap with a flat tyre was quicker than Rolls's race average. Rolls went through to victory with a trouble-free run and finished the race with 0.131 gallons of fuel remaining from the 6½ gallons that had been sealed in the night before. Percy Northey was less fortunate. He came into contact with Sulby Bridge and broke a front spring within the first hour. His telegram to Royce, 'Spring broken, heart broken', was more generous than Rolls's untypical suggestion of skulduggery when he broke his gearbox the previous year.

In the final month of 1906 Rolls visited America. He took Northey's TT car with him and demonstrated its speed by winning a 5-mile sprint for cars under 25hp at New York's Empire City speedway. By this time Rolls-Royce Limited was firmly in being, the classic 40/50 had made its debut at the Olympia show, and Royce and Haldenby were busy planning the move to Derby. When the factory was opened in mid-1908 it was one of the best-equipped motor manufacturing units in Britain – and it had a winning model to work on.

Top: The Tourist Trophy
Above: F. Gordon Crosby's
sketch shows Rolls heading
for victory in the 1906 TT,
passing a broken-down Argyll

Above: Rolls drives at speed during the 1906 Tourist Trophy
Above right: The winning team after the race: Rolls, Eric Platford and the 20hp

Top: The 1905 two-cylinder owned by Rolls-Royce. The first owner lacked the space to retire the car so gave it to the company. It is kept in full running order

The headlamps are a distinctive feature of this 1914 Ghost. The body dates from the 1920s and is by the Berlin firm of Schebera-Schapiro

CHAPTER 3

The Silver Ghost

Only 60 Rolls-Royce chassis were produced at Cooke Street, Manchester, in 1905 and C. S. Rolls and Company could have sold every one of them three times over. It was essential to increase production to meet the demand and thus enable Rolls and Claude Johnson to relinquish their agencies for imported cars and concentrate on selling Rolls-Royce, which received a big boost from Percy Northey's placing in the 1905 Tourist Trophy. A factory devoted to the manufacture of cars was now needed, especially as Royce's crane business required the room and resources taken up by car production. For these reasons Rolls-Royce Limited was registered as a separate company in March 1906 in preparation for the formation of a working company later in the year.

A new model, the 40/50hp, was ready in chassis form for the 1906 motor show at Olympia in November, the same month the board decided to increase the company's nominal capital from £60,000 to £200,000 and invite public participation. The directors were obviously as impressed with the car as the public were when they saw it displayed. The far-sighted Johnson recognized that the company's future, based upon Royce's intuitive design genius and the uncompromising standards of workmanship he set, lay in the rapidly expanding area of luxury cars. Lord Northcliffe had been right when, proposing vehicles like the Legalimit, he said that speed was being replaced in Britain by the demand for quietness and luxury, but he was wrong in thinking that people were prepared to travel at a maximum of 20mph.

In 1906 Napier, championed by S. F. Edge, led the luxury section of the market with their six-cylinder car, although they had to fight off a challenge from such notable four-cylinder marques as Mercedes and Panhard. Yet as early as 1904 there had been signs that the trend was towards sixes with Spyker, Durkopp, Maudslay, Wilson-Pilcher and Sunbeam offering cars having this number of cylinders. Royce agreed with Johnson. He had seen the reception accorded his own first effort in this direction and, by nature, was anxious to improve on it.

There is little doubt that the car Royce set his sights on was the Napier, and the 40/50 was a worthy rival. But he and Johnson did not make the mistake that Napier made. In 1906 Napier was offering two four-cylinder models, the 18hp and the 45hp, and two six-cylinders, the 40hp with a 4in × 4in engine and the 60hp with cylinder dimensions of 5in × 4in. Royce pitched his six-cylinder 40/50 neatly between these two, giving it a bore and stroke of 4½in. The square dimensions of the engine are not

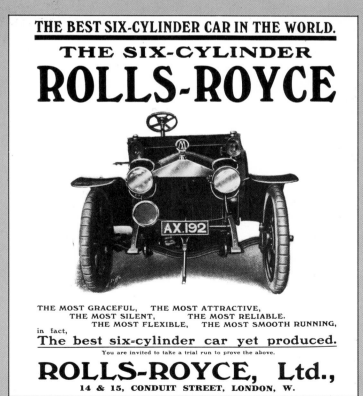

This was how the new 40/50 model was first advertised in Autocar *in 1907. In 1905 the company had advertised the 30hp as 'the best car in the world'*

The car named The Silver Ghost
is a much-travelled ambassador
for Rolls-Royce. Here it is shown
beside a 10hp two-cylinder of
1905, also owned by the company

particularly significant. Automobile engineers at that time thought that an engine's power output was directly related to the piston area and very little else, hence the Royal Automobile Club rating which became the basis for British taxation on horsepower. Only later was it generally appreciated that the power output of an engine was a function of the volume of air/petrol mixture that could be burnt efficiently. Strokes were then lengthened, partly to beat the horsepower tax and partly to keep the engines short, and engine speeds were increased dramatically.

The most significant feature of the new 40/50 Rolls-Royce was undoubtedly the crankshaft, a fact that the company tried to impress upon the public at Olympia by leaving off the sump and placing a mirror under the engine. The design of a crankshaft in the days of white metal bearings involved a series of compromises. A certain bearing area is required for each connecting rod to sustain the power impulses when the piston is pushed down by the process of combustion and pushed back on the compression and exhaust strokes. The forces involved in stopping the piston and connecting rod at the top of the stroke and pulling it back are equally great. If white metal is rubbed by the rotating crankpin at too high a speed it melts. Consequently designers in the old days made their crankpins long and thin and ended up with 'whippy' crankshafts which, even when they were supported by bearings between each crank throw, would wind and unwind like a torsion spring as the power impulses were fed into them. For this reason many early six-cylinder engines were abnormally long and even the relatively short ones were longer than need be because of the bearing area problem. That is why most of them had big bores, to use up the length, and short strokes, because short-stroke cranks are less 'whippy' than long-stroke ones.

This drawing of the engine of The Silver Ghost shows its configuration of two blocks of three cylinders. The cylinder heads could not be detached

Royce's solution was to pressure lubricate the crankshaft – most engines had splash lubrication then – to ensure a film of oil in the bearings at all times while using the lubricant to help cool the crankshaft. This was achieved by boring out the crankpins and journals until they were almost like very thick-walled tubes and closing the ends with little dished plates retained by tie bolts (aluminium plugs were used later). This way there was a large internal area in contact with the oil, which was in constant circulation from the relatively cool sump. As a result Royce could increase the journal and crankpin diameters substantially to give a crankshaft of almost modern dimensions, although it was never intended to run it at modern speeds. That would be the next step.

Engineers at that time debated keenly about the ideal configuration for a six-cylinder crankshaft but the conclusion most came to was that the best arrangement was to treat the engine as two three-cylinder units mounted back to back. If you were to take a three-cylinder crank and hold the end against a mirror that is what it should look like. When designed in this manner the crankshaft with the connecting rods assembled on it is in virtually perfect static and dynamic balance. When the power impulses act on it rhythmically, however, playing on it from one end to the other, it starts to wind and unwind along its length, like a torsion bar, at certain critical speeds to a degree dependent on its length and dimensions. Some of the long, spindly crankshafts in early six-cylinder cars were extremely prone to this phenomenon. Indeed, the first Daimler sixes were unsaleable for this very reason and the problem was overcome only by adding the Lanchester torsional vibration damper that was created for this purpose.

A 1909 tourer as drawn by Gordon C. Davies. This print was issued on the 300th anniversary of the founding of the Worshipful Company of Coachmakers

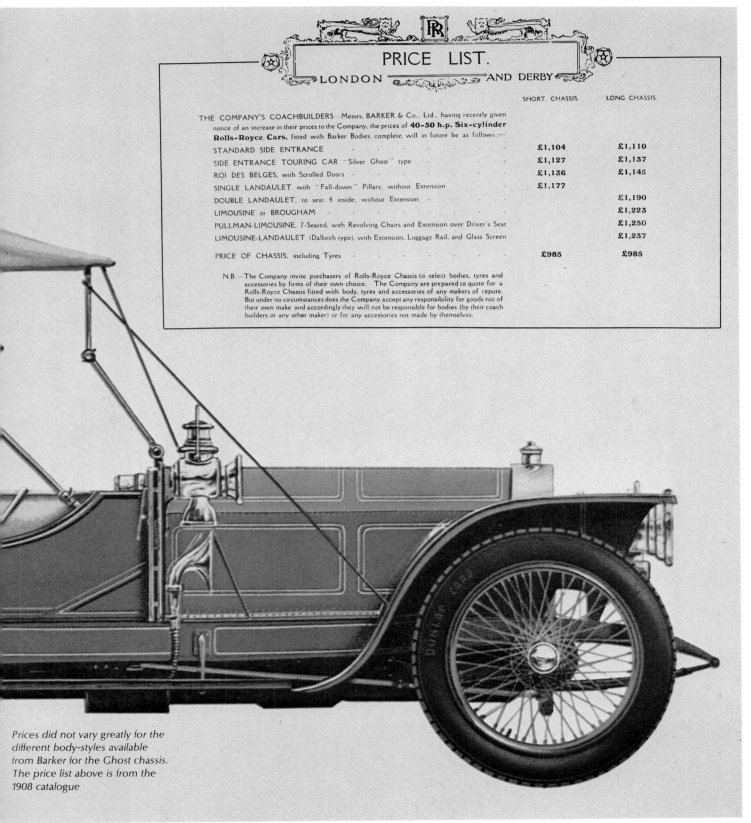

PRICE LIST.

LONDON AND DERBY

	SHORT CHASSIS.	LONG CHASSIS.
THE COMPANY'S COACHBUILDERS—Messrs. BARKER & Co., Ltd., having recently given notice of an increase in their prices to the Company, the prices of **40-50 h.p. Six-cylinder Rolls-Royce Cars,** fitted with Barker Bodies, complete, will in future be as follows :—		
STANDARD SIDE ENTRANCE	£1,104	£1,110
SIDE ENTRANCE TOURING CAR "Silver Ghost" type	£1,127	£1,137
ROI DES BELGES, with Scrolled Doors	£1,136	£1,145
SINGLE LANDAULET with "Fall-down" Pillars, without Extension	£1,177	
DOUBLE LANDAULET, to seat 4 inside, without Extension		£1,190
LIMOUSINE or BROUGHAM		£1,223
PULLMAN-LIMOUSINE, 7-Seated, with Revolving Chairs and Extension over Driver's Seat		£1,250
LIMOUSINE-LANDAULET (Dalkeith type), with Extension, Luggage Rail, and Glass Screen		£1,237
PRICE OF CHASSIS, including Tyres	£985	£985

N.B.—The Company invite purchasers of Rolls-Royce Chassis to select bodies, tyres and accessories by firms of their own choice. The Company are prepared to quote for a Rolls-Royce Chassis fitted with body, tyres and accessories of any makers of repute. But under no circumstances does the Company accept any responsibility for goods not of their own make and accordingly they will not be responsible for bodies (by their coach builders or any other maker) or for any accessories not made by themselves.

Prices did not vary greatly for the different body-styles available from Barker for the Ghost chassis. The price list above is from the 1908 catalogue

43

The sturdy crankshaft that Royce designed for the 40/50 was the 'mirror' type, which was new then but is now universal. Because of its generous scantlings, the short stroke and the fact that relatively little power was put through it, the 40/50 was free from the torsional problem until the stroke was lengthened at a later date when roughness crept in. This crankshaft, which really was way ahead of the times and would pass muster even today, was mounted on seven main bearings, the end ones and the middle one being twice the length of the intermediate ones so as to contain the 'skipping rope' effect now known to be peculiar to six-cylinder crankshafts. It is a measure of Royce's genius that in 1906 he sensed the problem.

Like the rest of the bottom end of the 40/50 engine the connecting rods were elegantly and generously proportioned and contrasted markedly with those of contemporaries, which were usually somewhat spindly. They were made from nickel-steel forgings and machined all over to reveal any flaws. The gudgeon pins were pressed into the cast-iron pistons.

Royce mounted this crankshaft in a crankcase that was almost a plain box stiffened by the partitions supporting the main bearings but devoid of ancillaries and complex shapes which cause distortion. To attain this he mounted the oil pump and distributor drive outside the crankcase, which was no disadvantage at all because it made them more accessible. The crankcase, which terminated level with the crankshaft centre line, was closed by a capacious sump.

The camshaft was, of course, housed in the crankcase, supported on seven bearings and driven by gears from the front of the crankshaft. It was typical of the standards set by Royce that these gears, hardened after machining, took more than 80 hours of handwork stoning to mate perfectly. In common with the Legalimit vee-8 engine the side-by-side valves, this time

parallel to the cylinders, were operated by idler levers that incorporated little rollers to prevent scuffing. The object of this arrangement was to relieve the valve stems of side-loads. For this reason the faces of the idlers in contact with the valve stems were profiled. Adjustable tappets were included in the specification and were considered something of a novelty at the time.

In the fashion of the day the cylinders were cast in two separate blocks of three with integral heads and ports. The art of making joints that would simultaneously hold back fire and water had yet to be mastered. Most, if not all, manufacturers of quality engines made the head integral with the cylinders and saved themselves much trouble by so doing. Access to the valves for grinding or replacement was through caps screwed into the head directly above the valves. A feature of the 40/50 blocks was that they were designed with massive apertures in top faces to ensure positive location of the cores in the foundry. Displaced cores can result in the cylinders being thick on one side and thin on the other and the water jackets the same. On assembly these holes were covered by cast aluminium lids retained by a multiplicity of studs and nuts.

The cylinders themselves were not held to the crankcase in the usual way, which was by studs screwed into the crankcase and passing through flanges in the base of the blocks. Royce did not agree with the practice of tapping studs into aluminium. He spaced his studs round the base of the cylinders where they went into solid iron and retained them with nuts inside the crank chamber. It was an ideal engineering solution but it did not make easier the chore of decarbonization – frequently required in those days – which usually entailed lifting the blocks. With labour at 1d an hour this was not of importance to a wealthy owner, but today it would be a major undertaking.

Opposite top: A 1910 Ghost with
Roi-des-Belges coachwork
Opposite: This Barker open-drive
limousine dates from 1911

Above: These paintings by Charles Sykes,
Arrival at the Covert-side (left) and
Arrival at the Meet, were reproduced in
the 1910 Rolls-Royce catalogue

Drive for the oil pump, high-tension distributor and water pump was provided by a jackshaft driven off the timing gears on the right-hand side of the engine. The water pump was driven off the end of it and the distributor and oil pump off the middle. These two vital components were mounted on the top and bottom of a vertical shaft driven by skew gears and housed in a separate casting. Oil was picked up from the lowest point of the sump and passed through external pipes to a long external oil gallery running along the bases of the cylinders. The modest size of the oil pump precluded a greater pressure than 10psi at the bearings, but it was capable of passing $4\frac{1}{2}$ pints a minute under working conditions. In addition to the feed to the main bearings there were pressure feeds to the gudgeon pins via the pipes on the connecting rods. After 1907 an oil spray onto the cylinder walls was added.

Up to 1907 Rolls-Royce cars had always been fitted with trembler-coil ignition with two accumulators, one of them a standby. On the 40/50 Royce went one better and gave it two separate ignition systems, one firing a set of plugs located in the exhaust valve caps and the other a set in the inlet valve caps.

To relieve the engine of any dependence on batteries one set was sparked by one of the new Simms-Bosch magnetos. The other set of plugs depended on a beautifully made Royce trembler-coil system which, following Georges Bouton, employed a cam-operated, platinum-pointed contact-maker to complete the low-tension circuit and a wipe contact distributor to deliver the high-tension current to the plugs. The stacked arrangement of the contact-maker and distributor, placed above the centrifugal engine speed governor, is reminiscent today of a modern distributor. The editor of the *Autocar*, who owned one of the TT Replica 20hp cars, remarked that Royce felt that the wipe contact he had used up to then gave insufficiently accurate timing.

A refined two-jet version of the very satisfactory Royce carburettor used on the early cars supplied the mixture through a long manifold that was fabricated from copper tube and gun-metal elbows. The manifold was intentionally long to procure ram effect and so aid slow running. Its inlet pipe led from the carburettor, mounted on the right-hand side of the engine, to the inlet ports on the left-hand side passing between the blocks. In many ways this unique instrument foreshadowed later

The 1911 tourer shown here has coachwork by Barker in the Roi-des-Belges style

constant-vacuum carburettors except that it had a fixed jet and a variable opening. The fixed jet had a tapered needle that set the mixture initially and was thereafter locked. It was located in a small venturi and set to give a relatively rich mixture for slow running. Alongside this small venturi was a second venturi and a weak jet controlled by a piston-operated valve. By means of suitable vacuum connections to the inlet manifold the piston was held up when the car was slow running and closed the second venturi. Once the throttle was opened the piston was progressively pushed down by a spring, thereby opening the extra duct and providing a large volume of correct mixture consisting of weak mixture from the bypass and rich mixture from the slow-running venturi. It worked admirably.

By modern standards the power output of the 'square' 40/50 engine with its 3.2:1 compression could hardly be called excessive. But the 48bhp it gave off at 1,250rpm was just below the peak of a very flat power curve and there was plenty of torque at 200 or 300rpm to pull the car along at 5mph in the sprinting' overdrive top, which gave 38mph when the engine was turning over at 1,000rpm. Most buyers were quite happy

with the speed range in top gear of 3mph to 60mph. At the higher velocity the engine would be turning over at a fraction more than 1,500rpm and producing about 50bhp.

It is worth pointing out here why motorists were so interested in top-gear performance. Until 1901 when Daimler, with the Mercedes, produced the first variable-speed engine, motorists had to control the speed of their vehicles largely by changing gear, hence the references to gearboxes having so many speeds. Lacking the facility to double-declutch and match the engine speed to the next gear they simply declutched and pushed the lever through when they wanted to slow down or go faster. The resultant 'gnashing of teeth' was accepted as part of normal motoring at that time. Panhard's reference to his gearbox – 'C'est brutale mais ça marche' – was nothing more or less than the truth. Nor was the apochryphal garage bill that read 'To draining gearbox and refilling with teeth' far from reality either. To the average driver in 1906 a silent gearshift was unheard of. Thus a car that had a wide speed range in top gear was infinitely preferable to one that had three or four set speeds with grating noises between. Royce's 40/50 could travel almost anywhere in top gear and would start off in second.

A 1912 double limousine by Barker. The body slopes to the rear, as shown by the roofline

While the general chassis design of the 40/50 was more or less conventional, being of the girder type, it took a step ahead of most of its contemporaries in having deeper than usual side-members and the engine mounted in the chassis rather than in the subframe. In place of the subframe, and ever-mindful of the flexibility of any engineering structure, Royce mounted the front of the engine on a linkage consisting of a pair of bell cranks, one per side, joined by a tie rod, which allowed the frame to flex as much as it liked without distorting the crankcase. Nickel-steel was used for all the main chassis members and all load-bearing brackets were attached by the special tapered bolts devised by Royce for the earlier cars.

The first few chassis had platform rear suspension consisting of two semi-elliptic leaf springs and a transverse half-elliptic like that used on the 30hp six-cylinder car, and semi-elliptic springs at the front. The wheelbase measured $135\frac{1}{2}$in and the weight a very modest $18\frac{1}{2}$cwt without tyres or liquids. Power was transmitted by a leather-faced, internal cone-clutch to the massive four-speed gearbox that now had a gate change in place of the quadrant type used earlier. The overdrive 'sprinting gear' was carried over from the 30hp but the gearbox was on a more substantial scale with both shafts carried on three bearings so that any two gears in mesh were always closely supported by a bearing.

The initial production fully floating axle had a straight-cut bevel final drive, but later on spiral bevel gears were employed. Axle location, apart from that provided by the rear springs, was maintained by a twin-tube torque stay anchored to the cross-member supporting the rear of the gearbox. Whereas there had been a number of plain bearings in the running gear

of the first series of Cooke Street cars antifriction bearings were used throughout on the 40/50. Braking was on the rear wheels only, by means of internal expanding drum brakes operated by the handbrake and a foot-operated transmission brake mounted on the gearbox output shaft.

With substantial financial backing available, a number of pre-production cars were built before any were delivered to customers. Johnson, well aware of the superiority of the 40/50 to practically everything else on the market, set himself the task of promoting it in his usual thorough manner. Two cars were set aside. One, chassis number 60551, the 13th to be built, was mounted with a Roi-des-Belges body by Barkers, finished in aluminium paint with silver-plated fittings and named The Silver Ghost. It was destined to establish the marque in the front rank of world automobile design and to give its name, unofficially, to the entire series of 40/50 side-valve Rolls-Royces. The *Autocar* sampled the car and on 20 April 1907 reported: 'The new Rolls-Royce has made its appearance in London. . . . The running of this car at slow speeds on the direct third is the smoothest thing we have ever experienced, while for silence the motor beneath the bonnet might be a silent sewing machine.' The vehicle was found to give speeds at 1,000rpm of 14, 22, 38 and 47mph in the gears.

A month later Johnson took the car on a 2,000 mile public test in company with a White steamer driven by Frederick Coleman. Observed by the Royal Automobile Club (as the Automobile Club of Great Britain and Ireland was now known) the test started at Bexhill, passed through London and took in the whole of the course of the Scottish Reliability Trial, for which

The Rolls-Royce mascot, Spirit of Ecstacy, made its debut in 1911. It was designed by the painter-sculptor Charles Sykes

With Claude Johnson driving and Rolls alongside, The Silver Ghost climbs a pass in Scotland during the 2,000 miles trial of 1907

Opposite: This 1911 open tourer features coachwork by Lawtons, a Liverpool company that built motor bodies from 1901

the test doubled as a reconnaissance. The section from Bexhill to Glasgow was made using only direct third and top gear and revealed a fuel consumption of almost 21mpg. At the end of the distance the car was stripped in the presence of RAC officials. The only wear to be found was in the planet pins of the differential and in the piston rings, which were loose in the grooves. Then the vehicle was reassembled for more serious business.

This was a 15,000 mile observed run starting from London in June and driving up to Glasgow whence The Silver Ghost would start as an official entry in the Scottish Reliability Trial. This completed, on its return to Glasgow it would be run night and day, excluding the Sabbath, until the 15,000 miles had been covered. In the Scottish trial The Silver Ghost won a gold medal and suffered its sole involuntary stop when the petrol tap shook shut. The dual ignition saved further involuntary halts. The

magneto, said to be an Eisemann, seems to have been consistently troublesome and was changed at scheduled stops. Rolls, Johnson and Eric Platford all took turns at the wheel in the runs between London and Glasgow after the trials had ended. The route included Coventry, Newport, Manchester, Bradford, Leeds, Durham and Edinburgh, towns that must have become very familiar to the crews during the five weeks of travelling. The 15,000 miles came up just south of Newport on 8 August and Johnson was able to wire ahead to order champagne for dinner with his press friends that night. Because of the petrol tap incident the 'no-involuntary-stop' distance amounted to 14,371 miles.

When the car was stripped by the RAC for mechanical examination it was found to have moderately worn parts only in the steering. The king pins and steering drop arm ball had both worn sufficiently to warrant replacement. And although it was not really essential the king pins and the drop arm ball were

During the 15,000 miles trial of 1907 The Silver Ghost and three other 40/50s halted at the Cat and Fiddle Inn near Buxton. Johnson is at the wheel of AX201; Rolls is in the driver's seat of AX205

replaced to bring the car to as-new mechanical condition. The drag link socket was refitted to suit the new ball joint. The magneto coupling was also refitted and the water-pump spindle repacked. Total cost of parts amounted to £2 2s 7d. Neither engine nor transmission showed signs of wear. The transmission's performance was of special significance for the controversy between the relative merits of live axles and chain drive was still going on. In a similar test to the one the Rolls-Royce had undergone a 40hp Wolseley-Siddeley used up two sets of chains in roughly the same distance.

Now that the 40/50 was in production and the factory at Derby being built Royce, working always from Cooke Street, set about refining the model. In 1908 the three-quarter elliptic rear suspension was introduced. It was obviously intended to improve axle location without losing the flexibility of the rather antique platform suspension that had been a throwback to the horse age. Royce consistently experimented with overhead-valve gear, in particular push rods and overhead camshafts (he was granted a patent on an overhead camshaft engine in 1910). During 1908 he experimented with an overhead inlet-valve engine that had increased compression ratio and was designed to run faster than the standard engine. Although this engine was a little too tremulous for the fastidious Royce it was ideal for the purposes of publicity.

Four cars were built with this engine. Two, named Silver Knave and Silver Rogue, were entered for the 1908 2,000 mile International Touring Car Trial. Driven by Northey, the Silver Knave won its class by a handsome margin. The Silver Rogue, with Johnson driving, broke a piston and retired. Brooklands track, just completed, provided a venue for a final speed test. Northey's aggregate times for the trial had been so good that he was able to motor gently round the track to average 53.6mph. It may have been an appropriate way to conclude a trial but it

This elegant vehicle with Victoria Touring coachwork was built for the Maharajah of Mysore in 1911. It was used in the main for ceremonial purposes

Overleaf: This car spent many years in Egypt but was originally sold to a French buyer. The 1914 chassis received its present skiff body with wooden boat-tail in the 1920s from Schebera-Schapiro of Berlin

was not the way to establish a reputation for speed. To demonstrate fully the cars' capabilities beyond doubt Johnson and Northey took both the Rogue and the Knave to Brooklands a month later and covered 20 laps under RAC supervision at speeds of 65.9mph and 65.8mph.

The year 1908 was a portentous one for the young company. With the Derby factory to equip it was essential to decide what models would be produced over the next few years. Johnson pointed out to the board that the demand for six-cylinders had increased, not fallen off, as a result of the controversy over the merits of six cylinders against four. Speaking against a proposal to add a new four-cylinder 20hp to the Rolls-Royce range he argued that it would be preferable to lower the price of the 40/50 than to produce it alongside a new four-cylinder model. On 13 March 1908 it was decided to standardize on the 40/50. (Number 13 played a significant role in the early history of the 40/50. The Silver Ghost was the 13th 40/50 to be made, it was first shown to the press on 13 April 1907 and the decision to standardize it was taken on the same date the following March.)

The one-model policy had its attractions from a marketing point of view but it was also advantageous financially. In January 1908, with expenditure on the new factory rising and the 40/50 only just getting under way, resources were being severely stretched and immediate support from the banks became necessary. It was in this climate of stringency that the Rolls-Royce factory in Nightingale Road, Derby, was opened by Lord Montagu of Beaulieu on 9 July 1908. Rolls-Royce declared a profit of £9,063 that year.

By mid-1908 Johnson felt that the company's competitive activities had served their purpose and should now cease. Yet neither he nor Royce could resist a challenge from Napier, made in 1911, to do a top-gear run from London to Edinburgh followed by high-speed runs at Brooklands without a change of gearing, the entire affair to be observed by the RAC. For this demonstration the most desirable of all 40/50s was conceived. On the London-Edinburgh model the compression of the 7,428cc engine was raised to the dizzy figure of 3.5:1 and a large choke carburettor built. In this trim the engine turned out 58bhp. It was installed in a special lightweight chassis with cantilever rear springs located under the axle and, for the first time, a tapered bonnet in place of the parallel-sided box that had hitherto encased the engine. On a final-drive ratio of 2.9:1 the car, driven by Ernest Hives, averaged 24.3mpg between London and Edinburgh and attained a speed of 78.2mph at Brooklands. By contrast the 65hp Napier used fuel at the rate of 19.3mpg and did 76.4mph on the track. Later in the year Hives took a lightweight London-Edinburgh chassis fitted with a single-seater body to Brooklands and covered the quarter-mile in a timed speed of 101.8mph.

This is the car that Ernest Hives drove from London to Edinburgh in top gear in 1911. Hives later drove a stripped-down model at Brooklands when he became the first to take a Rolls-Royce over 100mph

Two years prior to the Edinburgh run there were a number of engineering changes that coincided with the move from Manchester to Derby. The main one was to reduce the height of the frame to 24in measured from the top of the side-members. The adoption of three-quarter elliptic rear suspension in 1908 helped with this. Another major change was to a three-speed gearbox with direct drive on top. It had been found that owners insisted on driving in fourth gear which, being indirect, caused a slight whine. Overdrive was therefore dropped and the axle ratio raised a little to compensate. Hydraulic shock absorbers were also introduced for the first time.

Royce's illness in 1911 seemed hardly to affect the tempo of development of the 40/50 and the period up to the First World War was one of continual change. The long-stroke, $4\frac{3}{4}$in engine was first seen in 1909. Surprisingly the extra $\frac{1}{8}$in of crank throw incited a light torsional vibration in the crankshaft and caused Royce to begin experiments with wooden-centred flywheels to damp it out. A slipper flywheel was finally evolved. Mounted on the front of the crankshaft it effectively damped out the vibrations.

Other changes to the Rolls-Royce 40/50 were to torque-tube location for the back axle in place of stays, in 1911, simultaneously with the straightening of the droop in the middle of the front axle. There were also modifications to bearing sizes, which were progressively widened, and Bosch magnetos were adopted as standard. A major face-lift came in 1913 when the tapered bonnet, first seen on the London-Edinburgh car, was adopted for all models in conjunction with a taller radiator, giving the cars what would later be regarded as a distinctly 'twenties look. By

that time the rear suspension had been changed to cantilever springs, following the example set by Lanchester, and there was a new four-speed gearbox with direct drive top that arose out of experiences in the Alpine Trials.

The Alpine Trial story showed how circumstances could override decisions of the Rolls-Royce board. James Radley, a friend of Charles Rolls and a renowned pioneer aviator with nine aircraft designs to his name, had entered his 40/50 for the 1912 Austrian Alpine Trial. Climbing the steep gradient of the Katschberg Pass, four up, the car had baulked and refused to restart on its high bottom gear until the passengers got out and pushed. Not only did this lose Radley so many marks that he retired shortly afterwards — it hit Rolls-Royce on a particularly sore spot. The car proclaimed to be 'the best car in the world' had been beaten by a hill in a country where Rolls-Royce had only just set up an agency.

Johnson decided that something had to be done, and done quickly, to correct the bad impression created. Late that year a car was specially prepared and he and Jock Sinclair, a tester, took it to Austria to find out what had gone wrong. It did not take too long to discover that a 1-in-4 restart on a modest Scottish mountain was one thing; the same restart several thousand feet higher was something quite different. Among the many changes that emerged as a result of this expedition, which also revealed that the engine tended to overheat in these conditions, was the newly designed four-speed gearbox with direct drive top and an ultra-low bottom gear that would get the car away on any incline. This was eventually introduced as the Colonial gearbox.

Opposite: The team at the 1913 Austrian Trial.
From left, Hives (in coat), Platford, Parsons,
Sinclair, Radley and Friese

Above: The car that James Radley drove in the
1913 Austrian Alpine Trial took part in a
commemorative run in 1963

The next move was to prepare thoroughly a team of three cars for the 1913 Alpine Trial, plus a private entry for Radley, to prove to the Austrian buying public that Rolls-Royce cars were far more dependable than the 1912 trial had indicated. The most important member of this team would be Friese, the manager of the Rolls-Royce depot in Vienna, whose assignment was to complete the trial without loss of marks. Hives and Sinclair, the works drivers, were there to back him up. Platford, in charge of the team, rode as mechanic to Friese. Radley was independent but had support from the mechanics who accompanied the cars.

More than 150 modifications were embodied in the Alpine cars, which were based on the London-Edinburgh type. But many features were borrowed from the new Colonial model that the company was in the process of producing for sale in India. Power was supplied by a developed version of the 'Edinburgh' power unit with raised compression ratio and a large choke carburettor that enabled it to run up to 2,250rpm and give 65bhp. A larger, Colonial-type radiator was also fitted and, as a result of Sinclair's tests, a Royce-designed steam-separator was superimposed on the radiator cap. To ensure a reserve of fuel on long stages an extra petrol tank was mounted amidships and supplemented the standard 14-gallon reservoir. A last-minute modification, devised by Royce, was an Enots pump that drew petrol from the carburettor bowl and injected it into the induction manifold for cold starting.

The cars left Derby in company with support cars driven by Johnson and C. L. Freestone. The cars behaved impeccably in the trials although it was later agreed at Derby that they had been working close to their limit. Friese and Platford were the only Rolls-Royce crew to finish with a clean sheet. Sinclair's car was rammed by a non-competing Minerva, which bent the gearshift and left him with only third gear. Hives lost marks when his car stalled coming out of a *parc fermé* after an overnight stop. The team prize was won by Audi, although Friese carried off the Archduke Leopold Cup and six awards were shared between Radley and the other two Rolls-Royce cars. The most impressive feature, however, was the consistent high-speed running of the entire team, which was always minutes ahead of time, and showed the cars to be so superior to other competing vehicles. After the alpine success and until the war sales in Austria flourished and the company saw no point in further participation, although Radley entered again in 1914 and was the only competitor to finish without loss of marks.

The Alpine model was later marketed as the Continental, the first use of the model name so favoured by Johnson. He used to be angered if these cars were referred to as Alpine Eagles, the name coined for them by Hives in the experimental department. A variation of the Continental chassis became famous during the First World War with the need for armoured cars.

Preceding page: In 1925 Gustaf
Nordbergs of Stockholm made
this body for a 1921 chassis

Armoured cars were not built until long after the company had experienced something of a panic at Derby on the declaration of war in 1914. Johnson was convinced that there would be little call for luxury motor vehicles from an army that looked for mobility to mammals with four legs. The 100 chassis then in stock at Derby were offered to the War Office for VIP transport, the workforce was halved and those that remained were put on a 26-hour week. Johnson saw that the company's salvation might be found in aero-engines, so while contracts were arranged to build Renault air-cooled aero-engines Royce at St Margaret's Bay got down to designing the vee-12 unit that became known as the Eagle and would eventually establish Rolls-Royce as the premier British manufacturer in this field.

After the war a major change to the 40/50 involved the fitting of four-wheel brakes. These were first exhibited at the 1924 motor show at Olympia but the salesmen were premature and most of the cars delivered in 1925 were sent out with two-wheel brakes of the concentric pattern, introduced in 1914, that had concentric drums each with its own pair of shoes. The footbrake operated the more powerful outer drums and the handbrake, which was coming to be used more and more as a parking brake, was connected to the inner ones. Royce wanted a servo system because of the desire for light controls, and he found the germ of what he wanted in the Hispano and Renault systems. These used a drum clutch and a disc clutch respectively to

This 1914 Ghost was owned by a
South American family until 1970.
The landaulet body is by Barker

Top: The coachbuilders Hooper and company mounted this tourer body on a 1922 chassis

Above: This tourer dates from 1914. It is on display in the Turin Automobile Museum

transfer braking effort from a power take-off shaft on the gearbox. The system Royce and A. J. Rowledge arrived at was a combination of the Renault plate clutch and a much-improved version of the Hispano linkage. The prototypes were far from perfect but the system was carefully and systematically developed, Hives turning a deaf ear to the pleas of the salesmen, until Royce was satisfied.

One major deficiency of the Hispano system was the vicious action when going forward and the almost complete lack of response in reverse. W. A. Robotham almost lost Derby's Hispano when he tried to make a top-gear start on Porlock Hill and stalled the engine. Despite breaking the seat-back in his efforts to apply enough pressure to the brakes he had to bank the car in order to stop it. There was no such drawback to the Royce system. When the 'six-brake 40/50' underwent public test one assessor remarked that the brakes were so light that the car could be pulled up by merely pressing the pedal with the fingers. The brakes were equally effective in reverse. It is worth noting that the rear brakes were applied first and when the servo did act it applied the front brake relatively gently and further increased the rear braking effort. If the rear brakes locked the servo action stopped, releasing the front brakes for steering. The reason for this was that during development there had been trouble with front axle wind-up, and the engineers probably felt that the front axle should not be put under too much stress. Six months later, however, the press had something more sensational to write about with the introduction of the New Phantom engine for the 40/50.

The Ghost line at Derby in 1924.
In all, 6,173 of this 40/50 model
were built in Britain

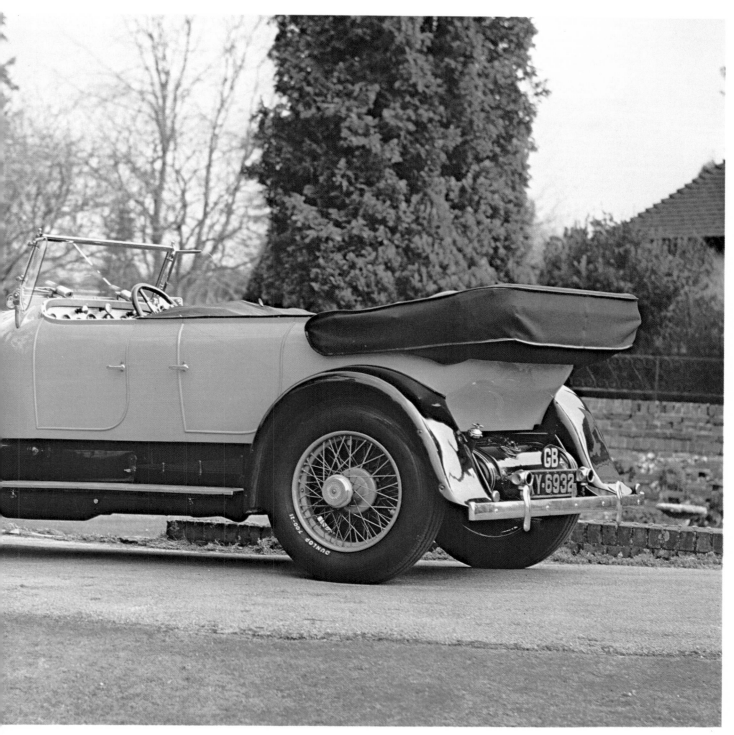

*A Barker-bodied tourer of 1925,
when production of the Silver
Ghost ended*

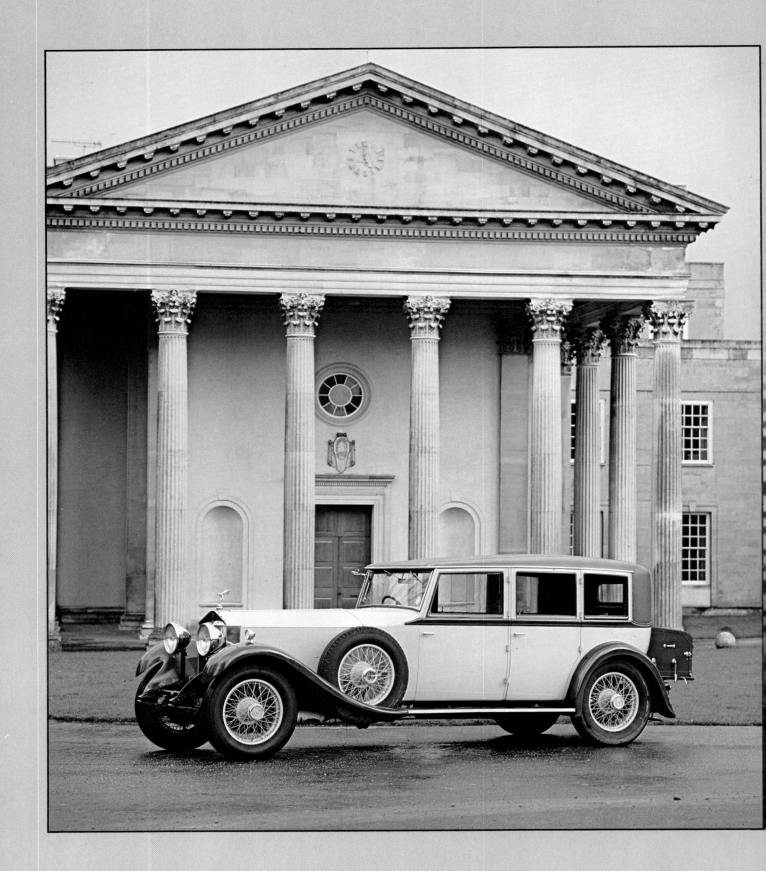

CHAPTER 4

Rolls-Royce of America

The decision by Rolls-Royce to manufacture cars in America was not made overnight. It is clear that even as Rolls-Royce Limited was being formed Claude Johnson was assessing markets other than Britain and saw in the United States an enormous outlet for high-quality cars. As soon as Rolls-Royce vehicles were in production and had proved themselves in the 1906 Tourist Trophy Johnson sent Charles Rolls to America to race Northey's 20hp and follow up by exhibiting 30hp cars at the 1906 New York motor show. This expedition went exactly to plan, Rolls driving the light 20 to victory in a 5-mile contest at the Empire City track in New York with a time of under 5 minutes 52 seconds. But the bridgehead he established started to collapse quite quickly because of a poor choice of representation, so in 1913 Johnson decided to go over himself to set up a proper sales organization controlled by Rolls-Royce. He returned to Britain impressed with the size of the market, its obvious wealth and the potential for luxury cars. But he had misgivings about the high import tariff of 45 per cent, even though Rolls had observed in 1906 that rich Americans would buy high-quality imported cars, tariff or no tariff.

Behind several of Johnson's decisions one senses his feeling of apprehension at what he believed to be a drift towards socialism and foreboding about the future of the British car market. It was one reason for the attempt to launch Automobiles Rolls-Royce de France in 1911. This manufacturing project was unsound economically and received little support but it did show that Johnson considered social trends a matter for concern. Even in 1913 he may well have considered making cars in America.

Opposite: A 1929 Phantom II with a chassis manufactured at Derby and bodied by Brewster as a Huntington sedan. Originally it was a Park Ward fabric saloon

This 1929 Phantom I was built entirely in America. It is an Ascot sports phaeton by Brewster. Phantom I production in the USA lasted from 1926 until 1931

The outbreak of war in Europe in August 1914 and the immediate worries for the future of Rolls-Royce in Britain temporarily banished these thoughts from Johnson's mind. After initial misgivings and drastic emergency measures the company moved quickly into aircraft engine production. When America entered the war in April 1917 she was desperately short of good aircraft engines and Johnson found himself once again in the United States endeavouring to set up a factory to manufacture the Rolls-Royce Eagle aero-engine. Car production there cannot have been far from his mind. One avenue he explored was a merger with Pierce-Arrow. He envisaged this company building Rolls-Royce aero-engines during and after the war. He believed that postwar demand would be almost as great as wartime requirements in a continent where air travel was increasingly seen as the logical solution to transportation over the long distances between major cities. He definitely foresaw Pierce-Arrow making Rolls-Royce cars for American owners and a reciprocal arrangement in which Rolls-Royce would sell Pierce-Arrow trucks through its sales network in Europe. But this project never gained the support of the Rolls-Royce board.

While in America during the war Johnson discussed the manufacturing project with J. B. Duke, the tobacco millionaire, who was believed to hold 15,000 shares in Rolls-Royce. Duke felt then that the company would be wise to have a stake in the American motor manufacturing industry. At the end of the war Rolls-Royce Limited found itself a more experienced, bigger and richer organization than it had been in 1914. Johnson's war settlement with the British ministry of defence, which went on at great length, ensured the financial underpinning of the company. Furthermore, Rolls-Royce was assured of a major share in the aero-engine business by being nominated as one of four official manufacturers in Britain.

Although complete Rolls-Royce Eagle aero-engines were not manufactured in the United States many components for assembly in the British engines were, but none were ready in time for combat engines. However, the small but experienced organization that Rolls-Royce had built up during the war proved an invaluable asset. There was Maurice Olley, a very fine engineer and an early associate of Henry Royce, who had gone over to America to handle problems associated with making Eagle spares. There was George Bagnall, another associate of Royce, who was in charge of a team of inspectors to supervise the work, and also Thomas Nadin, a senior executive of the British company. They were supported by Kenneth Mackenzie, an extremely able lawyer appointed by Johnson to handle the contractual work for the aero-engine manufacturing project.

Johnson returned to America in 1919 determined to get the car venture under way. It was not such plain sailing as he had hoped. J. B. Duke, approached a second time, now unexpectedly expressed misgivings. He pointed out that a British-built car could be sold to Americans at an inflated price simply because it was made in Britain and therefore exclusive; but an American-built version would have to be sold at a competitive price. Furthermore he did not like the proposed arrangement whereby finance for the American company would be raised locally but the firm would remain under the direct control of head office in Derby in return for the use of design, development and production knowhow. He advised the British company to raise the necessary capital themselves and a few years in advance of launching an American manufacturing project because he believed that a slump was not far off. Johnson, however, was committed to using American capital and English techniques.

40/50 Ghosts were made at Springfield, Mass, between 1921 and 1926. This 1921 Tilbury sedan has Rolls-Royce Custom Coach Work by Willoughby

Mackenzie considered a number of schemes, one of them from an employee of Duke who suggested an issue of 1 million shares, half to be preference and half ordinary, in return for manufacturing rights. Other offers came from A. B. Leach and Company and a consortium of Messrs Enseth, McLeod and Euhne, but neither was deemed satisfactory. Eventually the well-known New York financial house of J. E. Aldred made an approach. In view of Aldred's reputation for maintaining a close working interest in any company with which he was associated Johnson accepted his offer to raise the finance. Aldred had made his reputation in financial circles as a founder of Western Electric and had amassed a fortune building power stations. One of his associates in Western Electric had been L. J. Belnap, a large, tobacco-chewing Canadian.

Rolls-Royce of America Inc was formed in November 1919 with Claude Johnson as chairman, Belnap as president, Ernest Claremont as vice-president, Harry C. Beaver as treasurer and J. J. Macmanus, a partner in Mackenzie's legal firm, as secretary. Semour DeB. Keim was sales and advertising manager and Robert Schuette New York sales manager. Americans on the board of directors were Aldred, Belnap, C. E. F. Clarke and H. J. Fuller. Clarke was a close friend of Aldred and Fuller was one of his most able partners. English representatives were Johnson, Claremont, Royce and Mackenzie.

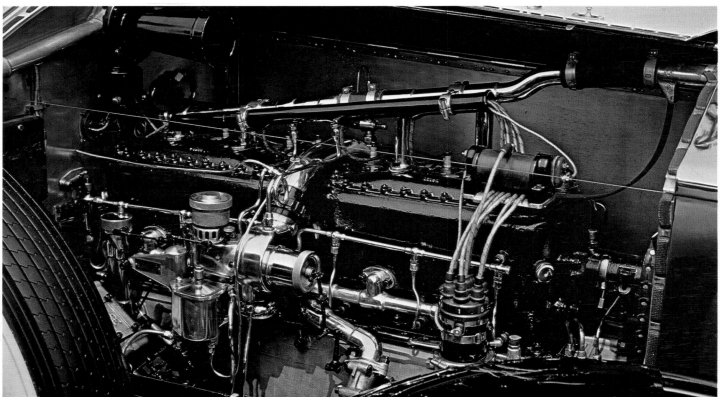

Top: A 1923 Pall Mall phaeton
Silver Ghost. The majority of
American body-styles had names
with strong British associations

Above: A Springfield Ghost
engine dating from 1923. At this
stage the engine for the Ghost
had a magneto and 12-volt coil

Authorized capital of the American company was $15 million split equally between preference and ordinary shares. Half the preference shares were issued to the public; the ordinary shares were held by a voting trust, the members of which were Johnson, Aldred and Claremont. The object of the trust was to retain a majority interest for Rolls-Royce of Britain. The prospectus issued by the new company spoke of producing 380 chassis a year with capacity to increase if necessary. It was proposed that the company should take over the Long Island service station which Johnson had established in 1913. Derby would supply full design and manufacturing information and vest their patents in the American firm; and the American company agreed to extend its influence outside North America.

A factory had yet to be found. Several sites were considered and these included two at Springfield and one at Williamanset. Springfield, Massachusetts, was favoured from the start because it was a centre of precision engineering with a pool of skilled labour and had been free from labour troubles. It was also close to New York and Boston, two of the wealthiest cities, and suitably distant from Detroit. As in Britain, Rolls-Royce liked to remain apart from the run of the motor industry. It reinforced the company's elitist image.

Of the two Springfield properties the Wire Wheel Works was near the city centre. The other, the Sumner property, was on the outskirts yet sufficiently close to attract labour. Originally built for the Hendee Manufacturing company, makers of Indian motorcycles, the Wire Wheel plant had been purchased by the Wire Wheel Corporation of America prior to the war. When this company moved to a new plant at Buffalo, New York, the factory had been taken over by the US Army as an ordnance store. Being of relatively recent construction and modern it seemed ideal, with a big, well-lit machine shop and five main buildings which leant themselves to use as erecting and assembly shops.

While the army stores were being moved out and new employees being hired the publicity department got busy. They announced that a limited number of Rolls-Royce chassis would be produced in America and that they would be identical to the Derby product. It was emphasized that production would be directly supervised by experts from Derby and that the materials would be the same as that used in the British cars. Accordingly 53 foremen and supervisors, together with their families, arrived in America from Britain. Thomas Nadin was made general superintendent and George Bagnall took on the job of works manager. Everyone worked like beavers and in July 1920 the first engines were assembled and fired up, although there were no chassis as yet to put them in. In order to fill the gap a number of chassis were imported from England to meet the demand, which had always been steady but was now increasing as a result of the publicity that attended the founding of the Springfield operation.

In 1914 the first Rolls-Royce car, chassis number 20151, a 10hp two-cylinder, had been sold to an American-born man, Paris E. Singer, a relative of the founder of the Singer Sewing Company. The first American citizen to buy a Rolls-Royce car in America was a Captain Hutton of Texas who bought the 20hp Tourist Trophy car from Rolls during his visit of 1906–07. After demonstrating the 30hp six-cylinder car at the New York motor show Rolls appointed Walter Martin, a New York distributor for Cadillac, as agent for the company. At the same time he obtained a licence under the Selden patent to sell Rolls-Royce cars in America. George B. Selden was America's equivalent of Harry Lawson in Britain but had been much more successful in gaining a stranglehold on the American motor industry. The patent required manufacturers and importers to obtain a licence from Selden before they could trade, but the situation was later challenged, and the patent finally circumvented, by Henry Ford in a lengthy court action. Martin placed orders for 17 cars – 30hp six-cylinders and some 40/50hp vehicles – and promised orders for 50 more.

Martin was not as effective as he might have been. Between 1907 and 1913 the main Rolls-Royce customer in America was Brewster, the Long Island coachbuilders who took several dozen chassis. When, in 1913, Johnson decided to breathe new life into the American distribution it seemed natural to approach Brewster as his chief American contact. It was equally logical that he should set up a service workshop in the huge Brewster building at Queensboro Bridge Plaza, Long Island City. As distributor he selected Robert Schuette, an agent for a number of coachbuilders whom he knew as the American representative for Barker of England. Schuette, who had premises at 326 West 54th Street, acted for Brewster and Fleetwood among others. Concurrently with the appointment of Schuette, James Royce, a cousin of Henry and who had been closely associated with the aircraft engine talks, was appointed Canadian representative.

Springfield-type wire wheels were distinctive because of the recessed centre of the hub nut

When the Springfield project was put in motion in the bitter winter of 1919–20 Rolls-Royce cars already had a presence in the United States although the quantity of Derby-built cars that had been bought by Americans numbered fewer than 500. During that winter an enthusiastic band of workers got down to clearing out the army stores from the works, installing new machinery and making jigs and fixtures. By the end of 1920 chassis were being assembled. At this point Ernest Hives went out from Derby with a typical, up-to-date chassis to compare the two products and to help solve engineering problems. American owners of Derby-built Rolls-Royces were replacing troublesome Watford and Lucas magnetos with more trustworthy American Bosch instruments. (The magneto had given trouble in The Silver Ghost during the 15,000-mile trial of 1907.) Derby had already investigated thoroughly an American Bosch magneto and reported adversely on it. Hives visited the Bosch plant and discovered that the magneto they had been sent in England was of a type produced down to a price for the replacement market and was not to be compared with Bosch's better products. Indeed, Bosch offered to build magnetos specially for Rolls-Royce and to submit them to any tests that the English company desired.

During this visit Hives also inspected the Bijur works and came away impressed. He reported to Derby that the standard of workmanship, inspection and efficiency which American manufacturers were prepared to provide was considerably higher than what Rolls-Royce could obtain from English suppliers. Even before he went to America Hives had inspected a number of US-made electrical components shipped to Derby and said that if they were as good as the manufacturers believed them to be they ought to be adopted on all Rolls-Royce cars. He believed that if Rolls-Royce Limited were to continue to make 'the best car in the world' the components would have to be of the best possible quality. And that quality would have to be uniform. The company could not countenance differing standards between Derby and Springfield.

Running the Derby-built chassis in America showed that it was not nearly as satisfactory there as it was in Britain. This was because of greater extremes of temperature and humidity, and the lower-grade petrol. The cars were sometimes difficult to start and required different carburettor settings. These and other factors prompted Hives to report back to Derby that the company should 'always have in mind that it is the results of the car in the customer's hands which we want to be identical. It is futile to have the cars look the same if, owing to variations in conditions, they give different results.' It is typical of the spirit of Derby at that time that Hives, as manager of the experimental department, could comment freely on manufacturing methods and costs and that the company took note of what he had to say.

This 1925 Pall Mall tourer carries Rolls-Royce Custom Coach Work by Merrimac

He observed that American forgings were cheaper and more accurate than those supplied in England. Chassis frames were not as expensive to buy across the Atlantic and, being heat-treated, were of better quality. He suggested that comparative costs of the two plants should be constantly monitored in all areas from raw materials through to the finished product. He remarked: 'I saw enough in the USA to realise that in all departments there is something to be learned from American methods.' In Hives's approval of American methods and products can be seen the foundation of the traditional regard the Rolls-Royce engineering departments have always had for American practice and equipment.

Hives was equally impressed by the quality of American coachworks. Obviously he had complete access to the Brewster plant. He commented that 'the best American bodies are better built and better finished than the English. They were made to more practical designs and have better fittings.' He considered the Smith Springfield coachworks to be far more up to date than Barker. Hives's report brought an end to the policy of identical product on which Springfield had begun and only the first 25 cars were identical to the Derby cars. Royce himself duly approved adoption of the Bosch magneto and agreed that, with handwork costing a penny a minute at Springfield, it was best avoided if equally good work could be done by machine.

While Hives was at Springfield Johnson was also in the United States, grappling with a financial crisis. The 1920 end-of-year results showed that the original estimate for the Springfield plant had been wildly astray. Differences between Aldred and the Derby board often became acute. Johnson found himself the referee, always loyal to his head office but frequently infuriated by their attitude and frustrated by his inability, because of distance, to make a personal approach. Briefly, Aldred approached Derby for an additional £400,000 of capital to see the Americans through their cash problems. But the British company, with a postwar recession just setting in, tax liabilities looming and the Twenty to get into production, were severely

restricted in the amount of financial help they could offer. Indeed, not only was the British company reluctant to help – it was equally reluctant to relax its control over the American operation. Throughout the Springfield episode the Derby attitude, which often reached the point of intransigence, was conditioned by the concern to protect their patents, drawings and engineering methods which, by agreement, were freely available to the American company. The solution finally arrived at was for Aldred to find the needed cash himself in the form of a 10-year debenture issue guaranteed by Rolls-Royce in England.

Chassis and bodies were imported from Britain until the Springfield venture got fully under way. In March 1921 output was around five cars a week, less than half the 12 forecast. The first chassis had been completed and delivered in January but a sales problem was already manifesting itself. Most of the imported Derby-built cars had been brought in fully bodied or else imported as chassis by Brewster, mounted with Brewster bodies and sold as complete cars. The Springfield sales organization soon found, however, that American purchasers (unlike the English) were not prepared to put up with the lengthy procedure of buying a chassis and then waiting to have a body built on it to their own specification. Rather than wait several months they wanted to see what they were going to get in the showroom, take a ride in it and have prompt delivery of an identical car with possibly a few alterations and own colour scheme. To meet this demand Schuette arranged for several coachbuilders to build bodies to stock designs. This coachwork

by companies such as New Haven, Smith Springfield, Biddle and Smart, Merrimac and others was then marketed as Rolls-Royce Custom Coach Work. The procedure worked very well and the bodies produced in this manner did credit to the coachbuilders concerned.

In the winter of 1921–22 significant management changes occurred which indicated the shift towards increased American capitalization. The negotiations between Aldred and the Rolls-Royce head office board at the beginning of the year had brought Johnson close to nervous breakdown. Moreover, Ernest Claremont, Royce's first partner, had recently taken ill. Shortly before his death his place on the board was taken by Claude Johnson's brother, Basil, and Belnap handed over the chairmanship of Rolls-Royce America to H. J. Fuller.

Springfield was well-endowed for making a superior automobile. Nadin, Bagnall and Ted Poole, the assistant works manager, were close associates of Henry Royce and had been thoroughly indoctrinated with his methods. They regarded the best they could do as not quite good enough and constantly strove for improvement. They did not have to worry about training labour, for Springfield was not only a centre of the American machine-tool industry – it was also a birthplace of the now-modern system of interchangeable machined parts. Jobs were not easy to find in 1922 so Rolls-Royce had the pick of the best and the men set about honouring the signs that read 'Let's beat Derby' and which hung in every shop. Arthur W. Soutter

Hibbard and Darrin mounted this unusual torpedo transformable on a 1928 Phantom I chassis. The company bodied 35 Phantom Is

recalls that the Derby-style discipline enforced by the British supervisors was harsher than the American workmen were used to, but it was accepted as part of the privilege of working for Rolls-Royce. Turnover in staff was low and Bagnall spoke admiringly of 'the high character' of American workers.

The way the cars were built was reminiscent more of machine-tool work than of automobile production as Americans knew it. An enormous amount of handwork went into every engine despite Royce's wish to keep it to a minimum. For example, the crankshaft, flywheel and clutch assembly was checked for static balance and corrected by filing before it was assembled into the crankcase. In the bottom end of the engine the main bearing shells were blued and scraped to give a precise fit in the crankcase housings. All the bearing-cap joint faces were scraped, and after the bearings had been metalled they were bored with hand-operated boring bars to minimize distortion, and finally hand-reamed. The connecting-rod big-end bearings received the same treatment. Despite the very low compression ratio, combustion spaces were carefully checked to equalize their volume and all cylinders were lapped after being bored.

An outstanding feature of Rolls-Royce cars from the beginning had been the extreme quietness of the gears. This had been achieved by careful design and painstaking hand-finishing. The timing gears were blued and stoned to eliminate high spots and all the transmission gears were handled the same way until gear-grinding machines became available. A typical English

The steering column side of a Springfield Phantom I engine of 1927. This engine had the same capacity, 7,668cc, as its Derby counterpart

Top: Door trim on a Brewster Phantom I Kenilworth sedan of 1930
Above: Solid woodwork, maroon cloth and gold-plated hardware are features of the doors of this 1927 Brewster-bodied Phantom

touch was the close-plated gear and handbrake levers. In Britain close-plating was a Birmingham trade and was unknown in America; it was widely used for the manufacture of brass bedsteads where thin brass sheet was applied over an iron base. Rolls-Royce of America imported J. Hailey, a Derby specialist, to do this work. The nickel-silver sheathing was cut by hand from .006in nickel-silver sheet, tinned on one side and soldered in place using a king-size soldering iron. Another Derby innovation was the steering-gear running-in rig. A weight was attached to the pitman arm and an electric motor, fitted with suitable oscillating mechanism, turned the steering from lock to lock until it was thoroughly run in and could be adjusted to nil-clearance.

Possibly the most notable example of the Royce quest for perfection regardless of cost was seen in the hand controls for the ignition and mixture. This job could have been done with readily available push-pull cable controls which Soutter recalls could be bought for about $1 a time. But Henry Royce would have none of these gritty devices. He preferred a series of beautifully proportioned shafts, bell cranks and push-pull rods all with carefully fitted moving parts. Not surprisingly this involved the manufacture of no less than 227 components, excluding fasteners. To tool these called for the production of 23 patterns and 22 drop forging dies which, with various jigs and fixtures, cost $69,000 in tooling alone; the cost of machining and assembling the individual parts was extra. The end result amounted to perfection, of course, with finger-light control completely free of backlash. But at what cost!

By 1922 the product was becoming more Americanized without loss of quality. It was in line with Hives's dictum that the car should perform in the customer's hands in the same way as the Derby-built car performed for the European buyer. To this end Bosch single-battery coil ignition had become standard alongside the Bosch magneto. The emergency oil tank had been done away with. Service stations were now so numerous in America that there was no question of a driver finding himself short of oil hundreds of miles from a source of supply. The cars now had fuel gauges but the filler was still on the wrong side for a road-side petrol pump. American wire wheels were fitted in place of the Dunlop equipment. They were more expensive to buy than the British ones but they were easier to handle in American repair shops. They featured the split rim which made tyre-changing much easier and a new type of hub nut that had a recessed centre lock.

At the end of 1922, with sales rising and a profit showing for the first time, it was decided to form the Rolls-Royce Custom Coachwork Organization. This happened at more or less the same time that Smith Springfield coachworks went out of business. Rolls-Royce decided to buy the premises of the defunct Knox Automobile Company and to build up their own

coachbuilding enterprise using many of the management and staff from Smith Springfield. Most chassis produced from the end of 1923 until 1926, when Rolls-Royce of America took a controlling interest in Brewster, were built by the Rolls-Royce Custom Coachwork Organization. This coachwork division was managed by a former Stevens-Duryea man, George Kerr, with Fred Doolittle as general superintendent. Among the bodies they produced were the very attractive Piccadilly two-seater roadster and the classic Salamanca with either a fixed or folding top. There was also the Arundel and Pickwick sedans with sliding or dropping divisions and the Pall Mall open tourer. These are just four body-styles that were fitted to Springfield chassis. A

Brewster mounted this windswept coupe body on a 1930 Phantom I chassis. This car was a special exhibit at the 1930 New York show

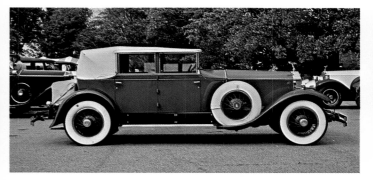

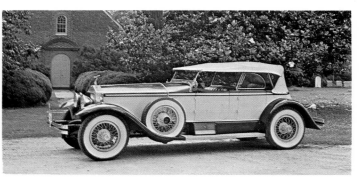

Top left: A 1929 Phantom I
Newmarket convertible sedan by
Brewster. The car has double bar
bumpers and bullet-shaped lamps

Top right: A 1929 Ascot tourer by
Brewster. Brewster bodied more
than 800 Phantom Is, far more
than any other US coachbuilder

vast range of body-styles were produced by American specialists who made arguably the most handsome of all bodies fitted to Rolls-Royce chassis in the 1920s. The Piccadilly and Henley roadsters were extremely appealing in design as was the Brewster York roadster – and the Playboy convertible, which was usually a rebody job when sales outlets found themselves burdened with unwanted limousines.

During its period of manufacture from 1921–26 the Springfield 40/50 became gradually more American in makeup under the design leadership of Maurice Olley. But the system ensured that development always lagged behind the English vehicle because of the need for the American drawings to be checked and approved, often only after mechanical tests, at Derby. Once approved, tools had to be made which alone could mean a delay of several months. In no area was this more apparent than in the fitting of four-wheel brakes. By 1923 most American cars had brakes on all four wheels yet here was an automobile, hailed as the best in the world, with brakes on the back wheels only. Fuller pressed Johnson for a change through most of 1923 but not until late October could Johnson inform him that Derby had agreed to a four-wheel system. As is well known, Derby had experienced real problems with the servo system evolved by Royce and had to do an expensive retro-fit. But they did get front-wheel brakes on the 40/50 late in 1924. The delays inherent in a major design change such as this meant that a four-wheel system did not begin production at Springfield until 1926, when it was too late to put it on the side-valve 40/50. No American-built 40/50 Ghost left the works with brakes on the front wheels.

One major change that did get through was left-hand drive. Some historians have expressed surprise that the first 1,000 Springfield-built 40/50s were produced with right-hand drive. They forget that throughout the interwar period it was normal for high-quality European cars to have the steering wheel on the right-hand side irrespective of the country of origin and the rule of the road. Cars such as Hispano-Suiza and Bugatti from France and Alfa Romeo and Lancia from Italy were all made with right-hand drive only. A number of reasons have been advanced for this. A rather dubious one is that right-hand drive made the more sporty cars like Bugattis and Alfa Romeos better suited for circuit racing where events were usually run in a clockwise direction over a course with a preponderance of right-hand corners. Another possible reason is that the better cars were normally used for long journeys, and any long journey in Europe involved crossing a mountain range. On the unguarded upland roads of that time it was advantageous for the driver to be able to judge just how near he was to the outside edge of the road – and a steep drop down the mountainside. Derby had never introduced a left-hand drive car, even though they sold many vehicles to European customers, for the very good reason that the cars they were selling against were all right-hand drive.

The owner of this 1930 Phantom Henley roadster wanted a car that was wholly distinctive so he had it made with copper panels

With the introduction of a left-hand drive option in 1925, a number of mechanical changes were made to suit the American market. Six-volt electrics had been introduced in 1924. Further to bring the electrics into line with American practice a twin-coil ignition system was fitted with dual distributors. This allowed both sparking plugs to fire at the same time right through the speed range and also left the magneto free to drive a Westinghouse generator. An important alteration brought about by the changeover was the need to build a little torsion damper into the generator drive to damp out crankshaft cyclic variations. Prior to this the generator had been driven off the gearbox, which was not ideal although it persisted on Derby-built cars. The main change, however, was the introduction of a new three-speed gearbox that was better suited to market requirements. Three speeds were sufficient for American customers, who shifted gear as infrequently as possible. This was heartily approved by Royce, who considered three speeds quite adequate and had designed a three-speed, centre-shift gearbox before the war. In addition the radiator's horizontal shutters were replaced with vertical shutters and the height of the radiator was increased to suit the high-waisted bodies fashionable in America. The change to left-hand drive was welcomed and 409 cars were delivered in the first year. Company earnings in 1925 amounted to $14.83 per preference share.

By the terms of the agreement between the British and American companies Springfield was required to introduce any new model that Derby produced. Fortunately reason prevailed when it came to the Twenty. If the agreement had been enforced it would have hastened the end of the Springfield operation, which was already struggling financially. The finances could never have been found to tool a completely new model. Moreover it was a car, as events proved, which would have been almost unsaleable in the United States. Only 35 Derby-built Twenty cars were exported to America during 1922–29 when the model was produced in Britain.

The ohv engine for the 40/50 New Phantom (later known as the Phantom I) was a different story. Springfield had to produce this car because, the agreement apart, they could not be seen to be building an out-of-date model. Phantom-engined chassis did not come off the Springfield line until late in 1926 because of the need substantially to retool the engine for left-hand drive installation. This entailed moving the complete induction and exhaust system from the left-hand side to the right-hand side of the engine to bring the carburettor onto the steering-column side so that it could pick up with Royce's beautifully engineered hand-control linkage. While this was being done 100 Phantom-engined 40/50s were imported from Derby to satisfy buyers who wanted the latest model.

A 1930 Derby tourer by Brewster, a company that was acquired by Rolls-Royce of America in 1926

Top: A 1931 Henley roadster by
Brewster. This car's chassis is one
of about 120 left-drive Phantom II
chassis that were made in
Derby for American buyers

Above: This Phantom I
Newmarket convertible by
Brewster dates from 1931, the
last year that chassis were
produced at Springfield

Despite the cost of introducing a Phantom I engine 1926 was the best year financially that Springfield enjoyed in its short history. The prospects at the end of 1925 and in 1926 seemed so rosy that the decision was made to acquire a controlling interest in Brewster, then in a perilous state. By clever manipulation Rolls-Royce gained control of the company without incurring its debts. As a result of this big gain in bodybuilding capacity Springfield was able to close the Rolls-Royce Coachworks Organization in Waltham Avenue and move some of the staff over to Brewsters. The company also closed its Long Island City service station and shifted the service department back into the Brewster building. At this time Rolls-Royce Renting was formed to rent cars in the New York area. A few months later the creator of Rolls-Royce Limited, Claude Johnson, who had kept so closely in touch with all that went on at Springfield, took ill and on 11 April 1926 he died of pneumonia.

During the next three years Phantom I production kept the company occupied, but on a decreasing scale. In America trade was generally in gentle decline. At Springfield the penalties of building expensive cars on a small amount of capital created a series of cash crises that left the company more and more in debt. The cost of tooling the Phantom engine had never properly been digested, matters were made worse by the introduction of the aluminium head for the Phantom and then, in 1929, came the Wall Street crash. That same year Derby introduced the Phantom II, an entirely new car that was quite beyond the financial capacity of Springfield to produce.

Circumstances came to overwhelm the American company. Because of the slump sales had dropped right back and even those people who could still afford Rolls-Royce automobiles did not wish to be seen driving around in one of the best-known symbols of luxury and wealth. Unable to produce the Phantom II the factory soldiered on, existing mainly by assembling aluminium-head Phantom Is from existing stock of parts. This work dwindled too, and attempts to find sub-contract work could not compensate. At Brewster the service division found it had a lot of empty space and used it for storing the cars of those clients who did not want to use their cars in the Depression. Brewster actually produced about 140 Brewster town cars, custom-built sedans mounted on lengthened and worked-over Ford V8 chassis, before it became apparent that Rolls-Royce of America would have to go into liquidation. At this point, to avoid the Rolls-Royce name being associated with failure, the company's name was changed to the Springfield Manufacturing Corporation on 29 August 1934. A year later the corporation filed a petition for bankruptcy in the US District Court, New York. In 1936 liquidation was formally ordered. All assets except cash and Springfield plant were sold to the Pierce-Arrow Sales Company of New York City.

Many factors apart from the Depression contributed to the demise of Springfield. One was the attempt to build a replica of the British product. It became extremely expensive because the machine tools in the American plant were different to those at Derby so therefore different jigs and fixtures had to be made. These jigs and fixtures had to be produced in a hurry in 1921 so that many were made at very great cost by outside contractors. This one factor was responsible for getting the project off on the wrong footing. It was also a mistake to insist on exact British specifications for all the steels used in the construction of the American car. The insistence by head office on exact specifications meant that special mixes had to be made and these were also very costly. The contracting steelworks would not have considered the job had it not been for Rolls-Royce. Even special hexagon bars had to be rolled to the English Whitworth standard rather than the American Society of Automotive Engineers dimensions. All this took time, was an unnecessary diversion of effort and needlessly expensive. Added to this was the fact that the company went into production with a car that was almost out of date.

When Dallas E. Winslow of Pierce-Arrow bought the assets of the Springfield Manufacturing Corporation he also bought without realizing it the right of access to all the Rolls-Royce drawings, methods and knowhow. It needed quick action by the British company to retrieve the situation. In a sense Winslow could be said to have achieved a merger of Pierce-Arrow and Rolls-Royce — something that Claude Johnson had tried to accomplish as a working arrangement 20 years before.

Interior of a 1930 Kenilworth
Phantom I by Brewster showing
distinctive skeletal trim with wood
lattice-work, rarely if ever seen
on British Rolls-Royces

Top: A 1932 Playboy roadster
by Brewster on a 1926 Ghost
chassis. The Playboy body was
fitted to out-dated limousine
chassis in the Depression

Above: A 1932 Phantom II
Keswick bodied by Brewster.
This particular model was a
town-car version of the
Huntington limousine

CHAPTER 5

From the Twenty to the Phantom II

As a result of Claude Johnson's negotiations with the British ministry of defence Rolls-Royce found itself in a financially sound position at the end of the First World War, but a fundamental matter gave cause for concern. It seemed clear to Johnson that despite the firm's enhanced reputation through its wartime work with the Eagle aircraft engine and the armoured car, he would have a difficult task keeping a big establishment going on sales of the 40/50hp motor car and the limited, if steady, income from the government aircraft development programme.

In the immediate postwar period the demand for cars far exceeded the supply and the company increased the price of the 40/50 chassis, which had cost £985 before the war, to £1,450. Sales were unaffected, and the increase was about average for the motor industry as a whole. Two years later the situation had changed completely. Large, Edwardian luxury cars had gone out of style and the trend was towards more efficient small cars produced in large quantities for the increasingly prosperous general public. By this time wages and material costs in Britain had risen sharply and Derby, like other factories, felt the effect. In December 1920 the price of the 40/50 chassis was further increased to £1,850 and the following June reached £2,250. These rises caused wholesale cancellation of orders; at one time the company had 300 unsold chassis in stock.

In order to retrieve the position the board asked Henry Royce to proceed apace with the design of a 20hp car of the same quality as the 40/50 but with a chassis price of about £1,500. The project was codenamed Kite and then Goshawk and it came at a time when the Springfield project was getting under way in America and making big demands on finance and time.

Royce must have considered the one-model policy irksome. Although it had been beneficial over so many years it now left the company with a large, Edwardian, side-valve motor car which, though good, was by 1922 a 15-year-old design. Yet Royce had not been idle. Almost as soon as the Ghost began production he had looked at the possibilities of the overhead-valve engine, and in 1910 he took out patents for an overhead-camshaft valve gear.

Opposite top: The Twenty appeared in 1922.
This drop head coupe by Compton was
mounted on a 1926 chassis at a later date
Opposite: A 1930 Phantom II sporting cabriolet
by Thrupp and Maberly

The success of the overhead-camshaft Peugeot in Grand Prix racing on the Continent had not escaped him. The 1912 Grand Prix de l'Auto Club de France had marked a milestone in Grand Prix car design when a 7.6-litre Peugeot soundly trounced old-fashioned GP monsters of almost twice its capacity. A smaller, 3-litre Peugeot of similar design to the larger car had been less successful in the 1912 Coupe de l'Auto races. In 1913 both cars were completely redesigned with gear-driven instead of shaft-driven camshafts and valves at an angle of 60 degrees in hemispherical heads. A 5.6-litre Peugeot to this design won the French Grand Prix at Amiens that year driven by George Boillot. The same driver in a 3-litre car triumphed in the Coupe de l'Auto at Boulogne.

Both these winning cars came to England and Royce bought the Grand Prix machine. Louis Coatalen of Sunbeam purchased the Coupe de l'Auto car and made a copy of it to run in the RAC Tourist Trophy race the following year. Royce thoroughly examined and tested his Peugeot before selling it to Charles Jarrott. He also had been able to take a close look at the Mercedes which won the 1914 Grand Prix de l'ACF at Lyon and came into his hands during the Eagle development programme. It was hardly surprising that at least one Rolls-Royce prototype should have twin overhead camshafts.

By the middle of 1921 Johnson was pressing for production of the Goshawk which was then running as the Goshawk I, with overhead camshafts, and the Goshawk II with a push-rod engine. Drawings of the Goshawk I engine show a cylinder head and valve layout with a great performance potential although power curves taken at the time indicate that it gave 53bhp at 7,250rpm. The relatively simple Ghost timing gear was hand-worked and consumed an enormous amount of labour. At Springfield an average of 84 hours was spent on the job. A camshaft drive would have had three times as many gears in it and would have been almost impossible to quieten on a production basis in a period when gear-grinding equipment was not generally available. Adoption of the push-rod power unit was logical.

The Goshawk, marketed as the 20hp and nowadays widely referred to as the Twenty, brought Rolls-Royce out of the Edwardian era and into the 1920s. In the year of its launch, 1922, it had a chassis price of £1,100; with a standard open tourer body the price was £1,590. Although there was nothing basically new in the car as far as automobile design was concerned it broke new ground for the company. This little Rolls-Royce with its six-cylinder, 3in × 4½in engine (3,127cc) was an eminently sensible conception executed with typical attention to detail. Despite the strictures on cost, economics were not allowed radically to influence design. In addition to the use of in-line push-rod operated overhead valves its novel features included a gearbox in unit with the engine and adoption of the so-called Hotchkiss drive with the back axle located entirely by semi-elliptic road-springs. This allowed the traditional torque stay or torque tube to be dispensed with so that the universally jointed propeller shaft revolved in fresh air. The use of a three-speed gearbox caused a few raised eyebrows and the fact that the gear shift and handbrake lever were in the middle of the car caused them to be raised even higher.

Royce explained that one of the aims of the designers had been simplicity. The object had been 'to spend as much money in the construction as can be done wisely, but not unnecessarily'. He went on to say that the chassis had been built and tyred to carry open and enclosed bodies with up to six seats, but he did not envisage bodies as large as those fitted to the 40/50. He pointed out that with a light body of modest dimensions the Twenty was capable of what he called a high road speed. In 1922 40mph was considered a fast cruising speed for the average driver. Few sporting motorists could maintain a steady 50mph, while 60mph was equivalent to 100mph today. With its light body the Twenty was capable of a little more than 60mph, but anything much above this took the crankshaft speed into the critical area.

It is worth assessing in depth the design of the Twenty engine because it displayed many features that were included in Rolls-Royce engines during the next decade and beyond. Innovations in construction as far as Rolls-Royce practice was concerned included the use of a monobloc cylinder casting (the best they had managed before was two blocks of three cylinders),

The sleek lines of the Phantom II Continental proved very popular. This 1932 fixed head coupe by Thrupp and Maberly was a 21st birthday present to the Aly Khan

a detachable cylinder head and in-line overhead valves. The block and head, both in cast iron, were mounted on a two-piece, light-alloy crankcase supporting the crankshaft on seven main bearings. The cylinder block was deeply spigoted into the top of the crankcase to almost half the length of the bores. This greatly increased the structural integrity of the engine and it allowed Royce to mount the camshaft high in the block and thus shorten the push-rods. Large apertures in the side of the block were provided to ensure accurate location of the water-jacket cores. The holes were closed by light-alloy covers.

A notable feature that persisted for 40 years in Rolls-Royce 'small' six-cylinder engines was that the cylinder centres of the front three and rear three cylinders were fixed at 4.15in. Although the cylinders were in one block the middle two cylinders were spaced to allow for a longer middle crankshaft bearing; because the carburettor was on the opposite side from the inlet ports it also allowed the induction tract to pass between the middle two cylinders. The lower half of the crankcase was formed by a deep, unribbed sump with cast, internal oil baffles and an integral oil-filter housing.

Royce claimed that the cylinder head arrangement was unique in that the push-rods were on the opposite side of the engine to the plugs. The advantage claimed for this was that it enabled him to locate the plugs well into the crown of the combustion chamber but out of the way of any oil leakage from the valve gear. As other people have found to their cost, however, the disadvantage of this arrangement is that the inlet and exhaust ports had to pass between the push-rods, and thus the inlet ports and at least two pairs of exhaust ports had to be siamesed. This is fine if not too much is expected from the engine in terms of power output but it precludes the use of separate inlet ports for high performance.

Great attention was paid to the design of the cylinder-head water jacket to ensure an adequate flow of water around the valve seats. The valves themselves were made from high-chrome-content steel which was very close to the austenitic quality obtained today. But no matter how much power the cylinder head of an engine produces the extent to which it can be put to use is determined by the crankshaft. Royce gave the Twenty a crankshaft similar in construction to that of the Ghost

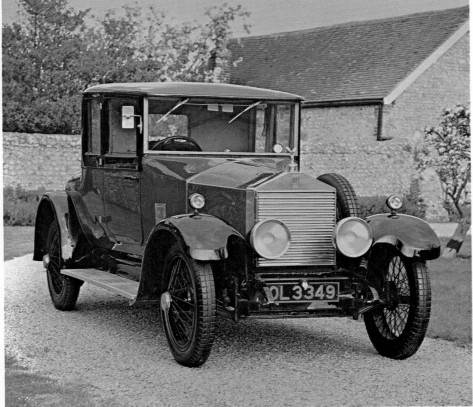

This 1925 Twenty coupe is by Barker. The body-style is often known as a doctor's coupe because of its popularity with the medical profession

with seven main bearings. As before, the journals and crankpins were bored out to add lightness and to make the most of the cooling effect of the oil-flow. Yet, with its original 2in main journals and 1½in crankpins, the crankshaft can only be described as spindly. In practice, despite the fitting of a slipper flywheel, the critical speed at which torsion vibration became more than the crank could stand was 3,300rpm, equivalent to 76mph in top gear. This speed was largely hypothetical because there was insufficient power to propel the car at this velocity in top, although of course critical speed could have been attained in the lower gears. The distributor failed to function a little below the critical speed and, as a warning to the driver, a thunderous flywheel resonance, incited by crankshaft 'nod', set in at 3,100rpm; most drivers did not press the engine further. Increasing understanding of crankshaft vibration allowed the 20hp crankshaft to be improved as time went on. Power development in the 20hp series is inseparably linked with the conquest of vibration, but in the end it almost doubled the engine speed and gave more than twice the power.

The connecting rods were equally spindly and not nearly as well proportioned as those of the 40/50. They were unusual in having the bearing metal cast directly into the eye of the rod. As was normal at Derby they were machined all over from an oversize forging and, like the Silver Ghost, had a separate oil pipe clipped to them to feed the little-end bearings. Aluminium pistons were standard equipment from the start and had clamping screws to retain the gudgeon pins. For the first time Royce dispensed with idler levers but retained rollers in the ends of the tappets to eliminate wipe contact. Screws and lock nuts in the tappets provided valve adjustment. Light springs kept the tappets in contact with the crankshaft. The relatively short push-rods were of small diameter and operated in ball-ended bushes in the valve rockers. The failing of this valve gear, and that of the subsequent New Phantom, was that oil drained out of the inverted sockets in the rockers when the engine was left to stand for any length of time and tended to cause wear on start-up.

A nice feature of the Twenty's engine was the extremely large diameter, fine-tooth helical-timing and ancillary gears that drove

Some splendid examples of the coachbuilder's craft were produced for foreign rulers. This 1926 Phantom I by Barker was made for the Nawab Wali-ud Dowla Bahadur of Hyderabad state, India. The body is aluminium

the generator and distributor. Both drives were fitted with miniature torsional dampers to protect them from the destructive effects of crankshaft vibration. The carburettor, as has been mentioned, was mounted on the opposite side of the cylinder block to the induction system. Mixture passed from one side of the engine to the other through a passage cast between the middle two cylinders and then upwards through an external manifold to the siamesed inlet ports.

Much had been learnt about cooling with the 40/50 Silver Ghost type which initially had been undercooled in hot conditions such as the hot and high Austrian Alpine Rallies of 1912 and 1913. The answer had been to increase the radiator size and give the car a more efficient fan, thus effectively over-cooling it for most conditions, and then to fit radiator shutters to cut down the amount of air passing through the radiator. The same principle was employed on the Twenty. Water was circulated, the opposite direction to which is now considered normal, by an engine-driven pump. The pump drew water from the bottom of

Top: This 1926 Twenty by Barker has a glass partition and a hood that is collapsible. It is from the collection of the Dutch National Automobile Museum

87

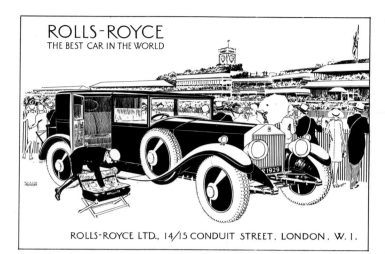

ROLLS-ROYCE
THE BEST CAR IN THE WORLD

ROLLS-ROYCE LTD., 14/15 CONDUIT STREET. LONDON. W.1.

the radiator, passed it over cool areas round the cylinders then circulated it around the hot, head area and returned it to the radiator top tank. A lusty draught through the radiator was ensured by a large fan driven by a spring-tensioned Whittle belt. Manually operated radiator shutters controlled the amount of air passing through and a prominently displayed temperature gauge on the panel kept the driver fully informed.

Electric lighting and starting had been something of an afterthought on the 40/50s but they were paid due respect on the Twenty. The abolition of the magneto had released a spare drive on the left-hand side of the engine. This was utilized for driving a generator like that on the Springfield Ghost. Hives had commented on the superiority of American electrical equipment and it is interesting to note that the Twenty's generator was either by Westinghouse or Rolls-Royce; the starter was a Bijur instrument operating on the flywheel.

In a reversion to Edwardian practice the engine was mounted in a U-shaped subframe rather than by the refined but expensive system of bell cranks employed on the 40/50. This subframe allowed Royce economically to mount the engine on three points and thus isolate it from chassis distortion, as he had done on the 40/50. Otherwise, although conventional in layout, the chassis frame was notable for its deep side-members, pressed from high-quality nickel-chrome steel, and for careful assembly using the Rolls-Royce system of square-headed taper bolts and nuts to fix the cross-members and brackets. This was by far the most satisfactory system available in the absence of suitable techniques for welding nickel-chrome steel. A frame built this way stayed tight for many years, as numerous owners of these cars have found nearly 60 years after they were built. Axle attachment to the rear springs was not by means of the usual U-bolts and dowel-pin location but through properly machined

*The Phantom II was introduced
in 1929 when this advertisement
was used to publicize the model*

housings keyed to the axle casing. Spring movement was damped by Rolls-Royce conical friction dampers.

The Twenty had a single dry-plate clutch which signalled the end of the cone-clutch at Derby. Its main difference when compared with present-day practice was that the friction linings were on the flywheel and clamping ring instead of on the driven plate. In the gearbox, as had become Royce practice, the main shafts were each carried on three bearings so that the gears were hard against a bearing when in mesh. Universal joints built by the company, with carefully hand-worked, hardened working surfaces, transmitted the drive to the spiral-bevel back axle. The inevitable fully floating back axle had a four-piece casing with steel trumpets and a light-alloy final-drive housing split on the centre line. For the first time Royce 'sewed' together the two halves of the final-drive casing with a multitude of small bolts. In common with the previous cars the nose of the bevel pinion was supported by an extra steady bearing to avoid deflection.

It seems strange that a car which first came onto the market in 1922 should have had brakes on the back wheels only. But even then a sizeable body of motoring opinion disliked four-wheel brakes. It was felt that they were too fierce, caused front-wheel slide and adversely affected the steering. Royce, although working on the problem, had not yet evolved a front-wheel braking system with which he was totally satisfied. So the Twenty came out with what the company called the four-brake system, which employed two concentric drums on each back wheel with separate sets of shoes – the outer ones operated by the footbrake and the inner ones by the handbrake. It was similar to the system that had been used on the 40/50 almost from the beginning and by reason of specially formed brake-shoe cams and Royce's bevel-wheel compensators in the cross-shafts it worked extremely well when judged by the standards that prevailed at the time.

On its appearance the Twenty found plenty of buyers for it offered the prestige of a luxury marque without the need to make too large a financial outlay. Two different chassis were offered: one for chauffeur-driven coachwork with an upright steering column, and one for owner-driver, open and enclosed bodies with a raked column and a set-back instrument board. Although Rolls-Royce were not yet in the coachbuilding business, nor would they be for many years, they could effectively offer a small number of standard bodies to designs drawn up by Ivan Evernden. One of the most popular was the tourer made by Barker and which cost £1,590. Alternatives included an open-fronted landaulet and an enclosed limousine with wide front doors and a division. Other coachbuilders provided a diversity of body-styles.

As far as the majority of customers were concerned the Twenty was a very satisfactory car. It was reliable and quiet and

*Opposite: Greta Garbo once
owned this 1927 Phantom I
torpedo. The body is by Barker*

handled well in spite of the minor theoretical disadvantages of the Hotchkiss rear-suspension layout. By the time production was underway a test depot had been established at Châteauroux, approximately 150 miles south of Paris. The standard test for the Twenty involved driving it flat-out on French roads – incredibly rough in those days – for 10,000 miles. Harry Grylls has said that the test usually ended at 9,000 miles with something breaking.

The Twenty really came of age in 1926 when it got an up-to-date four-wheel braking system that worked on the same principle as that of the bigger cars using Royce's gearbox-driven servo. At the same time, in response to popular demand (although Royce himself persistently maintained that the car did not need it), a four-speed gearbox was introduced with right-hand change. And the handbrake lever was moved over to the right alongside the gear lever. These two fundamental improvements raised the chassis price by only £85 from the 1922 value. By that time too, the crankshaft was in the process of being tamed, more power was coming from the engine, and although road tests carefully avoided mentioning maximum speed it would seem to have been 70mph with appropriately light coachwork.

Back in 1922, in view of competition from top-class makers such as Hispano-Suiza, Napier, Lanchester and the up-and-coming Bentley, the decision had been made to replace the 40/50 side-valve Silver Ghost with a new car having an overhead-valve engine and a redesigned chassis. Design work was slowed by enforced preoccupation with other things. In 1923 the American Navy had entered a team of racing seaplanes at Cowes and carried off the Schneider Trophy, which had been won the year before by a British Supermarine flying-boat. The Curtiss D12, light-alloy, V12 engines that powered the American machines were far ahead of anything being made in Europe. Napier soon received an approach from the British government to build engines on the same lines, but the company declined, believing that their Lion engine would be adequate for many years to come. So the contract went to Rolls-Royce. This project was primarily the concern of A. G. Rowledge but Royce was also involved, which slowed progress on the 40/50 replacement.

In 1924 the Ghost was 17 years old and just about to receive four-wheel brakes. With or without them it was out-dated. The Twenty had been well received at first but sales later flattened off and the combined income from the two models was barely sufficient to keep the company alive. A further burden was incurred in changing over to a four-wheel braking system which was offered at no increase in chassis price and the expense of converting 600 cars that were already delivered. Something was needed to boost sales. That something was the New Phantom engine for the 40/50, officially announced in May 1925.

This 1926 Phantom I was owned by Queen Wilhelmina of the Netherlands. The body is French

Generally the New Phantom engine was an enlarged, twin-ignition version of the Twenty's power unit with minor structural differences and many refinements. With a bore and stroke of $4\frac{1}{4}$in × $5\frac{1}{2}$in giving a swept volume of 7,668cc it was a quarter of a litre bigger than the Ghost engine although it had a smaller bore and because of this paid less excise tax. There were a number of improvements over the Ghost engine. The generator was now part and parcel of the engine assembly, the ignition had automatic advance and retard with manual override, and it had a new induction system that brought the carburettor to the same side as the inlet ports for the first time.

The main structural departure from the Twenty was that the cylinders were cast in two blocks of three. They were bridged by the one-piece, cast-iron cylinder head, which had the two plugs mounted side by side in roughly the same position as the single plug on the Twenty. A good deal of trouble was experienced with the cast-iron heads if the car was driven hard. On such occasions the engine tended to run-on and 'pink' on anything but the best fuel. After 700 engines this was overcome by fitting an aluminium head that had plugs on opposite sides of the engine. It permitted a high compression ratio and gave more power, although the company was reticent about how much. Output varied probably between 90 and 100hp depending on the type of cylinder head. The crankcase extended so far up the cylinder walls that it was necessary to mount the tappets in a second deck below the top face of the crankcase. This in turn called for crankcase inspection covers so as to enable the tappets to be adjusted or replaced. On British-built cars, looking from the back of the engine, the right-hand drive from the timing case was responsible for the coil-ignition distributor, engine-speed governor, the dynamo and the magneto. The left-hand drive had the easy task of driving a relatively small water pump.

Royce's concern with detail was nowhere more apparent than in the design of the automatic advance and retard mechanism operated by the engine-speed governor. The advance and retard on the magneto required a different angular movement from the coil-ignition distributor head in order to keep the two plugs in each head sparking in unison. He co-ordinated them mechanically with a system of levers, employing a movable fulcrum operated by the hand control on the steering wheel. This acted up to a certain point in the advance range; thereafter a hydraulic system, energized by engine oil under pressure and controlled by the engine-speed governor, took over. The whole system was built with watch-like precision and gave complete freedom from backlash.

Equal attention to detail could be seen in the valve gear. This had a second adjustment for tappet clearances which could be made with the engine running. It was achieved by mounting the rockers on eccentric bushes that could be rotated by a miniature worm and sector gears. Royce arrived at a more

modern induction system by bringing the carburettor to the same side of the engine as the cast-aluminium induction pipe. It incorporated drain lines from the inlet manifold back to the float chamber and an exhaust-heated venturi. The little starting carburettor that had appeared on later versions of the side-valve Ghost engine was also to be found in the New Phantom, as was the Autovac petrol feed tank which superseded the gearbox-driven pressure-fed system on the Ghost late in 1924 when four-wheel brakes were introduced.

No major changes were needed in the Ghost chassis to accommodate the new engine, although the engine mounting simplified the expensive bell crank and connecting system used previously. The new model had a simple tubular frame with a single mounting point on the front of the crankcase. Friction dampers prevented undue twist and rocking. The engine was still not in unit with the gearbox, which was driven by a short shaft, the drive then passing through the long, tapered torque tube.

Right: Rolls-Royce advertising was angled at people with refined taste – and money. This example dates from 1934
Opposite: A Twenty tourer by Barker from 1929, the last year the model was made

All Derby-built New Phantoms had four-wheel brakes. Wire wheels were fitted as standard at first with straight-edge tyres and later, in 1927, with balloon tyres on well-base wheels. Royce favoured wire wheels, which he considered aesthetically ideal. He objected to the heavy looking aluminium wheel-discs so popular at the time. Most people nowadays would agree, but anyone who has had wire wheels on everyday cars will know how difficult they are to keep clean. One feels for the chauffeurs who persuaded their masters to fit easily cleaned discs.

The 40/50 New Phantom (or Phantom I as it is commonly known now) was until recently one of the least sought-after vintage Rolls-Royce models. During production, however, it was well thought of and much in demand. It was supposed to perform better than the side-valve 40/50, but when Claude Johnson had a special open sporting body fitted to the fourth experimental chassis it was found on test to be more than 4mph slower than the 1911 London-to-Edinburgh Ghost. This discovery led to an investigation into the effect of weight and aerodynamics on maximum speed; a test at Brooklands was included and the wings, wheels and head-lamps were successively removed in between speed tests. Using these results Evernden designed a much modified body. This car, 10EX, which is now in the Stratford Motor Museum, was persuaded almost to the 100mph mark.

Two chassis lengths were offered on production New Phantoms: $190\frac{1}{4}$in being standard with a $196\frac{3}{4}$in version for formal coachwork. Typical bodies on the short chassis were Barker tourers or owner-driver saloons. Chauffeur-driven limousines, landaulets and sedancas-de-ville by all the fashionable coachbuilders were to be found on the long chassis. Some of the short-chassis, owner-driver saloons had a very sporting appearance, manifestations of a persistent interest in what Johnson liked to call Continental models, although this does not appear to have ever been an official title for a New Phantom.

Johnson never saw the Continental theme fully developed for he died after a short illness in 1926, aged 62. Johnson's role in the success of the company had been of crucial significance. As we have seen, Rolls lost interest in the venture soon after Rolls-Royce Limited had been formed; and without Johnson's concern for the welfare of the chief engineer, Royce would have worked himself into his grave before the First World War. Johnson had inherited from his father a love of art and music; Ambrose McEvoy was his favourite artist and Debussy his favourite composer. Whilst fearful of the effects of socialism on the progress of the company he was yet responsible for the appointment of worker-directors in the early 1920s when such an arrangement was extremely rare in Britain. During the war he had almost killed himself with overwork while getting the Eagle aero-engine into production in both England and the United States. Although he ruffled the feathers of high officials in Whitehall he was yet offered a knighthood but turned it down. His place was taken by his brother Basil and then Arthur Sidgreaves took over as managing director.

Competitors made inroads on the Rolls-Royce market in the late 1920s. Although the Napier challenge had died when that firm renounced car production to concentrate on aircraft engines, Rolls-Royce encountered stiff opposition from Daimler with its six-cylinder and V12-engined models. Bentley Motors were taking significant business from the company in the owner-driver market as well as with 'express' limousines. W. O. Bentley had early set his sights on the Rolls-Royce clientele. One well-known story tells how, when testing a $4\frac{1}{4}$-litre, six-cylinder car in France in 1924, Bentley chanced upon a prototype New Phantom under test. The resultant race convinced him that his $4\frac{1}{4}$-litre six would be unable to challenge Royce's new car, so he designed the $6\frac{1}{2}$-litre Bentley which, from its inception in 1926, took business from Rolls-Royce. It was not only faster than the Phantom but also handled better and was equally quiet. And Bentley achieved what Royce had failed to do: he had designed a silent drive for an overhead-camshaft valve gear using an ingenious double-eccentric drive. In 1929 Bentley announced his magnificent 8-litre which was a 100mph car with heavy

This 1928 Phantom I saloon limousine by Hooper was built for Otto Oppenheimer. It had a secret compartment for carrying diamonds. Accessories, including the radiator, are silver plated

limousine coachwork; at that time the lightweight New Phantom was struggling to do 90. Fortunately for Rolls-Royce, Bentley Motors went into liquidation in 1930 when Woolf Barnato withdrew financial support. The Derby firm hurriedly bought up Bentley to prevent a rival takeover by Napier.

To meet this challenge in the protected home market and to face effective competition from cars such as the Hispano and Isotta-Fraschini on the Continent, not to mention Cadillac, Pierce-Arrow and Duesenberg in America, Rolls-Royce in September 1929 announced the Phantom II. At the same time the Twenty was uprated to 20/25hp status, with many mechanical changes, to produce the best-selling Rolls-Royce prior to the Second World War.

The Phantom II was the first completely new car from Royce's drawing board since the Twenty seven years earlier. It followed closely the same general configuration as the smaller car especially in the chassis arrangement with semi-elliptic springs at all four corners and Hotchkiss drive. Following the pattern set by the Twenty the engine was built in unit with the clutch and gearbox. Innovations for Rolls-Royce (somewhat overdue, considering the progress in automobile design) included a starter motor operating on the engine flywheel and set in motion by a sequence switch, constant-mesh gears, and a hypoid-bevel final-drive. Much that was traditional remained, such as the engine-speed governor and dual ignition. On this second Phantom engine the range of synchronization between the coil system and the magneto was further widened. Provision of a rubber-insulated body subframe enabled coachbuilders to build bodies as the chassis was being erected, thus saving time.

Apart from problems associated with early cast-iron heads the New Phantom engine had given little cause for complaint except perhaps for its dismal lack of power, even with the later alloy head. One can hardly regard 100bhp from a 7.7-litre overhead-valve engine as impressive, even though it was produced at under 3,000rpm. The engine of the Phantom II, though based on the crankcase and crankshaft of its predecessor, had a much greater power potential by virtue of a

A 1930 four-seater Phantom II tourer by Barker. Production of the Phantom II lasted from 1929 until 1935, during which time more than 1,700 were built

cross-flow cylinder head, cast in aluminium, with separate inlet ports and a modern design of induction manifold. At the time of launch, standard compression ratio was 4.75:1 but shortly afterwards this was raised to 5.25:1. Power output at the start of production was probably of the order of 120bhp at 3,000rpm with much more to come if the roughness associated with raising the compression ratio could be tolerated.

The crankshaft was sturdier and the main castings were all new. As before the cylinder blocks were cast in units of three and were spigoted into the crankcase. The gear-driven ancillaries were rearranged and more evenly distributed with the dynamo and magneto on the left-hand side of the engine and the distributor and water pump on the right. Even at this late date the engine-speed governor was retained, mainly because owners liked to be able to set it like a modern speed-holder and maintain a constant speed up hill and down dale irrespective of load. Hydraulic actuation of the advance and retard was retained in improved form and was to all intents and purposes fully automatic, although the usual overriding hand control existed. The second control on the steering column quadrant was a mixture control for the Rolls-Royce two-jet carburettor with a water-heated venturi but it later used exhaust heating.

Internally the engine now had a full-flow lubricating oil-filter and a full-pressure lubrication system that normally ran at 25psi. It supplied oil at this pressure to the crankshaft, big ends and gudgeon pins. Relief valves reduced the pressure to 1psi for valve-gear and timing-case lubrication. Two years later cylinder lubrication jets were standardized. A special vacuum pump operated the Autovac and made it independent of manifold depression. The decision by Royce to adopt Hotchkiss drive was a logical one. In theory the old suspension system using cantilever springs reduced the unsprung weight but this was nullified by the need to use a heavy, tapered torque tube to steady the axle. The new hypoid axle allowed a lower floor line on limousine bodies.

For the first time a Rolls-Royce engine was mounted solidly to the chassis instead of being carried in a subframe. It was no doubt done to stiffen the front end of the frame and prevent what the experimental department called 'jellying' – wheel wobble brought about by the installation of front-wheel brakes on the Edwardian Ghost chassis. It just so happened with the older design that the weight of the brake drums combined with the natural bounce frequency of the tyres to provoke abnormal wheel wobble at high speed. This was one reason why the

Opposite: A 1934 Phantom II
Continental by H. J. Mulliner. This
particular model is very rare as the
body is one of only a handful that
were mounted on a long chassis

Above: The interior of the 1934
Phantom II Continental shown
opposite displays the
restrained elegance for which
Rolls-Royce were famous

company refused to authorize the use of balloon tyres. Wobble was so bad that on one test the front wheels touched the ground only every 11ft or so. A very clever feature of the front suspension of the New Phantom and Phantom II, introduced in an attempt to eliminate front-wheel wobble and prevent axle twist on braking, involved the use of shock absorber levers as radius arms and connecting them to the chassis.

A very practical innovation on the Phantom II chassis was what is called one-shot lubrication although, in fact, at the beginning it comprised three separate systems. A spring-loaded plunger lubricated all the chassis bearings except those on the axles. The front axle and rear axle joints were lubricated by two grease nipples, one on the front and one on the back. A few years after the introduction of the car the Derby engineers overcame their reluctance to use flexible pipes for this job and a complete chassis system under Luvax-Bijur patents became standard. Another change for the better was to replace the old concentric rear brakes, which had an inner handbrake drum and an outer footbrake drum, with new-style brakes having wide drums and two sets of shoes side-by-side. The need for this was prompted by the increasing inability of the old-type handbrake to hold the car on steep hills.

Changes to the transmission which brought it right up to date involved building the clutch housing and gearbox in unit with the engine, using a single dry-plate clutch, and redesigning the gearbox and placing the layshaft below the main shaft instead of alongside it. The open propeller shaft was still of Rolls-Royce manufacture with oil-filled universal joints. The fully floating back axle was also made in Derby. Gleason hypoid-bevel gears were used for the final drive. Compared with the earlier model the car had a taller radiator in Staybrite stainless steel.

Despite the cost of producing an intirely new model with a better specification the chassis price remained steady at £1,900. On the introduction of the Phantom II at the 1929 Olympia show only two competitors' chassis were more expensive. The straight-eight Duesenberg cost £2,380 and the six-cylinder Mercedes-Benz 38/250 cost £2,150. Both these prices included a 30 per cent import tax, however. The Phantom II was offered with a five-seater close-coupled saloon by Barker at £2,935 or a Hooper limousine on the long chassis at £2,960. The two chassis lengths came with wheelbases of 144in and 150in.

The Phantom II's immediate sales success was no doubt helped by the introduction of a left-hand drive version from Derby, primarily to satisfy demand from Springfield, but it also found favour in Europe. The Rolls-Royce success in the 1929 Schneider Trophy race brought valuable publicity and once more gave the company a sporting image. Henry Royce's meetings with the pilots of these machines and with other sporting personalities must have strengthened his yen for sporting vehicles and probably helped inspire the Phantom II Continental model.

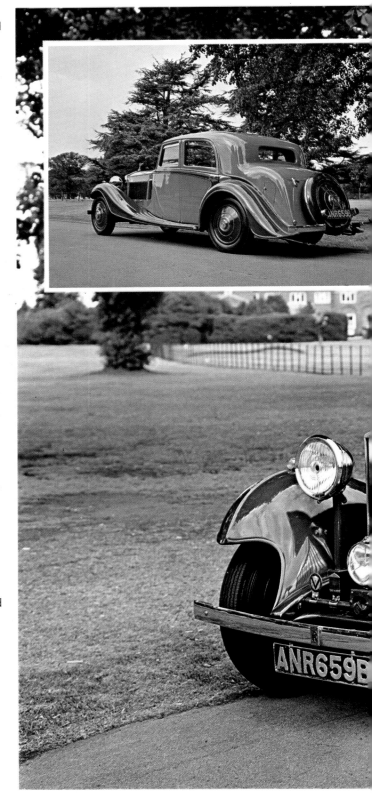

This 20/25 sports saloon by Gurney Nutting displays flowing lines that make for a very fine-looking motor car. The vehicle dates from 1934

When Royce wanted to build a car that the salesmen did not rate highly he simply specified one for his own use. He had always had a penchant for close-coupled cars on the pattern of the Riley Nine. The first experimental Phantom II, 18EX, was in the Riley idiom with the rear-seat passengers moved forward and leg room found by slightly sinking the floor. The car Royce wished 'for his own use' was an extension of this principle with firmer springing, a shorter chassis and a tuned engine. Ivan Evernden has recounted how Royce sent him to Guildford to buy a Riley Monaco saloon. He was instructed to buy it in his own name and not that of the company. The car was then driven to West Wittering, taken apart and the body carefully measured. The design team then modified the chassis to take deep foot-wells and five-leaf instead of four-leaf springs to give it a more sporting ride and more precise handling.

It would appear that the Continental was no more than a short-chassis version of the first prototype Phantom II but with five-leaf springs and a 12/41 axle in place of the standard 11/41 unit. It had a lower floor, a low-rake steering column and Hartford remote-control shock absorbers that were later replaced by Rolls-Royce remotely controlled hydraulic dampers. It seems certain that the Phantom II was designed from the outset to take close-coupled coachwork. The spare wheels were moved from the running-boards to the back of the car. This would only have been done to offset the change in weight distribution brought about by shifting the rear-seat passengers forward. The prototype Continental Phantom II was delivered to Royce at West Wittering and was finished in metallic Saxe blue, a finish produced in those days by overlaying the paint with a lacquer containing finely ground herring scales. After this preliminary viewing Evernden took the car to the Continent for a publicity tour. It is not on record that Royce ever drove it.

Rolls-Royce had only recently acquired Bentley Motors when the Continental model was introduced. Seen in that light the Continental was an appropriate replacement for the 8-litre Bentley owner-driver saloons. It was a good performer although not as fast as the Bentley. Timed speed over half a mile at Brooklands was recorded in 1933 at 92.31mph; acceleration from rest through the gears to 60mph took 19.4 seconds. The men of the technical press who tested the car enjoyed the advantage of synchromesh gears on third and fourth which came two years after the model was launched. The Continental lacked the surge of power of the 8-litre Bentley engine but there was sufficient to make it a very pleasant touring car with a good ride.

It is as well to stress here that smoothness is a relative term. In comparison with modern cars pre-war Rolls-Royces (and any of the classic makes for that matter) feel chunky and rough; this, and the amount of scuttle shake, reminds the modern-day driver of the big advances in chassis and body design that have taken place in the intervening years.

The 20/25 model, introduced in 1929, used the Twenty chassis virtually unchanged. Engine performance was improved by increasing the bore from 3in to $3\frac{1}{4}$in and raising the compression ratio to 4.6:1 and then to 5.25:1. At that time a new crankshaft was brought in, which allowed the engine to run up to 4,000rpm on test; 3,500rpm could be used safely on the road. A new system of balancing the crankshaft made this possible, and reducing the thickness of the flange between the crankshaft and the flywheel rim eliminated flywheel resonance. Improved performance, allied to better looks achieved with a higher, stainless-steel radiator, a level bonnet and narrow hub wheels resulted in a high level of sales. Autocar reported in 1931 that on the 20/25 'every single feature spells durability' and that 'the machine is on a plane altogether superior to the normal style of motor car'.

Top: H. J. Mulliner bodied this 1934 Phantom II drop head coupe with wheel discs.
Above: A 1934 20/25 sports saloon with division by Barker

It is worth looking briefly at some of the main changes made to the Phantom II during its period of production, from 1929 to 1935. True one-shot chassis lubrication came in 1931. The engine mounting was changed to a diamond configuration a year later when, non-consequentially, an Auto-Klean oil filter was introduced. Synchromesh on the upper two gears and a silent second gear marked a real step forward late in 1932 but second-gear synchromesh had to wait until 1935. Luvax-Bijur lubrication for the chassis, introduced in 1933, was concurrent with engine changes that included a nitralloy crankshaft, high-life cams and a 5.25 : 1 compression ratio. Also in 1933 remote-controlled dampers came in, 700 × 19 tyres replaced the 700 × 20 type and the braking balance was biased more to the front. By the time production of the Phantom II ceased in 1935 more than 1,700 had been built.

Another beneficial change was a shift towards lighter coachwork and the eventual abandonment of the heavy body subframe. Barker had been the 'official' coachbuilders to Rolls-Royce since 1905 but by the 1930s the bodies they built were becoming too heavy. One day Royce noticed a body with slim windscreen pillars. It was by a new coachbuilder, Park Ward. When approached by Evernden this company was found to be uncommonly flexible and cooperative. Park Ward accepted suggestions for new methods of construction which increased rigidity and saved weight. A close working arrangement quickly developed between the two companies. Barker bodies continued to be mounted on Rolls-Royce chassis but starting with the second Continental prototype Park Ward took over most of the experimental body-work. It was an association that held important consequences for the future.

This 1935 20/25 sedanca de ville is by Fernandez and Darrin. It was displayed at the 1935 Paris motor show and purchased by Lady Davis of Montreal

CHAPTER 6

Phantom III to the Wraith

When the 30-mile, triangular course for the 1931 Schneider Trophy race was laid out in the Solent the most easterly turning point was located on the beach at West Wittering within sight and earshot of Elmstead, Henry Royce's English home. Royce was then a sick man and was confined to his bed at the time of the race, but he could hear the dull rumble of his R-engine taking the slim Supermarine monoplanes to victory. Less than two years later he returned from his winter convalescence in the South of France to spend his last days in England. He died on 22 April 1933. He had been awarded a baronetcy in 1930, following Britain's win of the Schneider Trophy in 1929, and in 1931 the winning aircraft was also powered by Rolls-Royce engines. Ernest Hives and the team at Derby, urged on by Royce, later built the engine that transported man for the first time at more

than 400mph. In his lifetime, therefore, Frederick Henry Royce had witnessed the progress of mechanical transport from the steam locomotive, through the development of mechanically propelled personal transport to the conquest of the air. He had designed one of the finest cars of the Edwardian period and gone on to build outstanding aero-engines that had taken man on his first direct crossing of the Atlantic in 1919.

Royce's career as an engineer had indeed been a remarkable one. Although he was regarded as what we would nowadays call a 'boffin', surrounded by a mystique that was carefully nurtured by Claude Johnson, he was not only a practical, hard-swearing engineer but a good businessman whose advice was sought by the company on all major issues. His expressed views were sound and very much to the point.

Above and opposite: A 1937 Phantom III sedanca de ville with a sliding steel roof. The body of this car was styled by Saoutchik and built by Hooper

A poignant memo sent by Royce to the West Wittering design team on 11 November 1932, less than six months before his death, crystallized his thoughts on design. It was headed 'Car – Work – Designs' and warned against the dangers of working too quickly. It is reproduced here in full, exactly as Royce dictated it to his secretary.

> I want to emphasise the idea that in our present practice it is not a question of getting through quickly a large amount of design work so much as is that the designs must first of all function really reliably. *Chapter 1* Now I think we are pretty good at this, but it always means that modifications will be needed with the present high duty, and when the searching testing is finished. We must expect this, and it will generally be found that after these tests have been conducted the whole thing may need to be redesigned, and therefore tools and expensive patterns should not be made in the first case. All this you understand quite well.
>
> *Chapter 2* What I want to impress freshly upon your minds is that the designs shall be worked out with the greatest simplicity, and somewhat more crudely, than in the past. The general impression is that I am the author of too many frills about the design, but our older work does not support this view, and I have struggled for years to *eliminate* every feature possible in the design so long as we satisfy Chapter 1.
>
> *Chapter 3* Now it is likely that in the future you will have less help from me, and I can already see that the designs have more pieces, are less direct in method, more little screws, and less practical construction, and it is with this impression that I write this note. It will be understood that any problem that comes to mind should be undertaken if it promises not to involve impractical complication, but rather have too few than too many gadgets, and do not promise to furnish designs to meet every requirement, whim, or fancy, of enthusiastic buyer, salesman, critic etc., or we shall always be in trouble, and fail to please anyone.

Clearly he saw that the end was near and was somewhat apprehensive about the standard of design after his departure. By this time moves were under way to concentrate car design in Derby. With Royce in France A. G. Elliott and Charles Jenner hurried to stake their claim without informing Royce. Predictably the old man was upset when he heard. He told the other members of his team that they could go to Derby if they wished but, with typical loyalty, they remained with him until his death.

W ork began on a replacement for the Phantom II in 1932. Throughout the company's history car design in the United States greatly influenced Rolls-Royce thinking, and engineering executives made regular journeys across the Atlantic to keep abreast of latest developments. In the early 1930s there had been a marked swing in America to engines with more than six cylinders. In-line eight-cylinder engines had become prosaic by 1932 and the trend was towards vee-engines with 12 cylinders and, later, even 16. Maurice Olley had already designed for General Motors his classic independent wishbone suspension

which was destined to revolutionize suspension design worldwide. W. A. Robotham visited America in 1932 and called upon all the major manufacturers in Detroit. Impressed with what was being done he returned to Derby and before long work on a successor to the Phantom II began. Robotham learned about the V16 Cadillac then in preparation and was forcibly struck by the plethora of V12 engines appearing as the top model of most American manufacturers. He and Royce also knew that Hispano-Suiza, the traditional Continental rival, had announced their model 68 with a light-alloy, V12 engine. Bearing in mind their experience with V12 aero-engines and the V12 New Phantom prototype it was logical that Rolls-Royce should chose this configuration for the new model, and by then they had had wide experience of light-alloy construction. Any new model would have independent front suspension to keep up with the Americans and put Rolls-Royce one jump ahead of Hispano. When Royce died the main outlines of the new car were firmly established although most of the detail had yet to be completed.

Preparation of the new model, codenamed Spectre, was less hindered by financial pressures than had been the case with previous 40/50 models, because the burgeoning aircraft engine business was beginning to profit from the effects of the British government's reaction to political events in Germany and the re-creation of the German Luftwaffe. This development, and the absence of Royce's insistence on simplicity and practicality, are likely reasons for the designers' producing what turned out to be the most complex, and difficult to service, car the company had ever built.

Opposite and above: The 25/30 model was introduced in 1936, a year after the Phantom III. This example from the first year is a drop head sedanca coupe by Salmons. The boot opening is a noteworthy feature

Top: This 1937 Phantom III saloon by H. J. Mulliner started life as a limousine. It was later reworked to its present style by the original coachbuilder

Unveiled at the 1935 Olympia motor show, the new 40/50 was the most technically advanced car in production anywhere in the world, and it was arguably the best made. The main features of this Phantom III were the V12, ohv engine with one-piece aluminium alloy crankcase and cylinder blocks and cast-iron, wet cylinder liners and aluminium head. The extremely rigid, cruciform-braced box-girder chassis had wishbone front suspension and semi-elliptic rear springs. The drive to the hypoid rear axle was through a separate four-speed gearbox, with synchromesh on the top three speeds. No effort had been spared to make it the ultimate in refinement. It broke new ground for a British car in having hydraulic, self-adjusting tappets, and hydraulic shock-absorbers controlled from the driving seat. The centralized chassis lubrication, which had first appeared on the Phantom II, had been further refined.

Although the wheelbase had been shortened to 142in the chassis weight went up 240lb to 4,050lb. Combined with the 12-cylinder engine it resulted in greater fuel consumption. Not that this mattered greatly to potential buyers of a car costing £1,850 in chassis form alone. This price may not seem high these days, but it represented nine or 10 years' wages for a skilled workman in 1935, or about £40,000 in today's money. Nevertheless the new model cost only £50 more than the much less complicated Phantom II. It would seem that the company had made a handsome profit on the older model and was prepared to sell the new car at severely reduced margins and allow the smaller Bentleys and the newly introduced 25/30hp, both of which sold briskly, to subsidize production of the top-of-the-range model.

For the technically inclined the Phantom III stood out at the motor show despite the attractions of the Hispano-Suiza, the 12-cylinder Daimler and a new straight-eight, push-rod engine from the same manufacturer. Transatlantic influence was evident in the general layout of the unit, which had the cylinders inclined at 60 degrees and a single camshaft, located in the cleavage of the cylinders, operating the valves through push-rods. The cylinder dimensions of the 7,338cc engine were the same as Ford's Lincoln V12. American inspiration stopped there. All the US engines had cast-iron blocks and most had side-valve heads. To find a parallel with the new 40/50 one had to look to the Hispano-Suiza engine which had the same light-alloy combined crankcase and cylinder blocks and inserted wet liners.

The cast-iron cylinder liners of the new Rolls-Royce were sealed by rubber rings. The lower seal was duplicated, with a vent to atmosphere between these two seals to allow leaking coolant to drain away rather than enter the engine oil. The six-throw crankshaft was carried on seven main bearings and had the traditional slipper flywheel. Each opposing pair of pistons shared a common crankpin. Aero-engine practice was evident in the design of the connecting rods which were of the fork and blade type. The fork rods were clamped to circular bushes which ran on the crankpins while the blade rods ran on the bushes. The advantage of this was that the two cylinder blocks could be exactly opposite each other rather than being staggered as were those of the Hispano-Suiza, in which the connecting rods ran side-by-side on common crankpins. The Rolls-Royce layout meant that the full bearing surface of the crankpins was utilized

Windovers, founded in the late 18th century, mounted this sedanca de ville body on a 1936 Phantom III chassis. The Phantom III was produced from 1935 to 1939

The Wraith was an extremely refined model. The 1939 two-door saloon shown above was bodied by James Young in the 'razor-edge' style so popular at the time

for each cylinder and the engine could be made that fraction shorter because of the absence of cylinder stagger. The cylinder head was of light alloy with aluminium-bronze valve seats and brass plug inserts screwed into the head in the manner already established on the Phantom II.

All the ancillaries were gear-driven, with the exception of the fan. The seven-bearing camshaft, with 24 lobes, had a spring damper incorporated in the driving gear. It was driven indirectly, through the medium of a plastic idler wheel inserted in the interests of silence. The hydraulic tappets used engine oil pressure to extend them and maintain correct tappet clearance while the engine was running. This British Rolls-Royce 40/50 was the first to have no magneto. Instead two separate coil-ignition systems each fired one of the plugs in each cylinder. In theory they were mechanically synchronized, or rather de-synchronized, because there was a slight lag between the firing point on each pair of plugs in order to promote flame propagation. This trick had been used successfully on earlier Phantoms. Lubrication was on accepted principles but with special attention paid to filtration in view of the tight tolerances and small orifices found in the hydraulic tappets. An interesting innovation was a heat exchanger located between the oil and cooling systems and mounted on the side of the crankcase.

Olley's influence was strongly evident in the design of the front suspension. Olley had evolved a semi-trailing, unequal-length wishbone configuration – the top wishbone was roughly half the length of the lower one – which gave outstanding results and a much improved ride even with 'cart spring' rear suspension. Royce and Elliott, close friends of the former Rolls-Royce man, had studied Olley's design in detail. The geometry of the Phantom III suspension was practically identical to that which Olley had designed for General Motors, but it was more refined in that the coil spring which acted as the suspension medium was mounted horizontally and inside an oil-filled reservoir in company with the shock-absorbers and operated by a lever mounted on the inboard spindle of the upper wishbone. To go with this suspension there was a worm and peg type steering box in which the steering worm engaged a grooved roller mounted on the sector. All the shafts were mounted on roller bearings. Steering motion was transmitted via a pair of bell cranks, mounted on the front suspension cross-member, to a split track rod. Rolls-Royce had yet to find a hydraulic brake system compatible with their gearbox servo and had designed a mechanical system of rods and levers of some complexity to prevent suspension movement being transmitted to the front-wheel brakes.

For the first time a Rolls-Royce chassis had completely boxed side-members. They were swept over the back axle and braced by a large cruciform bracing amidships, inside which the gearbox was housed. Although the frame side-members were welded

structures the cross-members were attached by means of the traditional tapered bolts and nuts. The front of the frame was braced by the very rigid U section of the independent suspension subframe and by a tubular cross-member. Rear suspension was on long, semi-elliptic springs enclosed in oil-filled gaiters and damped by Rolls-Royce hydraulic shock-absorbers, the stiffness of which was regulated according to the speed of the car by a gearbox-driven pump. An overriding control on the steering column could mollify the effects of this arrangement if the driver found the ride too hard. A new feature for Rolls-Royce was the presence of an anti-roll bar on the rear suspension. The gearbox was mounted separately from the engine, a reversion to earlier practice. This was done so that a weighty component could be moved back in the frame to compensate for shifting the engine and radiator forward of the axle and so that a short propeller shaft could be used which would be less liable to become unbalanced.

This handsome 1938 Phantom III sporting limousine is by Hooper. The engine, shown above it, has 12 cylinders set in a vee and a capacity of 7,338cc

Ten prototypes were built. The later ones were mounted with finished bodies and offered to the press when the car was announced in the autumn of 1935. One was tested by *Autocar* a year later. Its best timed speed over a quarter-mile was found to be 91.84mph with a mean maximum of 86.96mph. Acceleration from rest to 60mph through the gears took 16.8 seconds; 70mph could be achieved in 24.4 seconds. This was not an inconsiderable achievement for a car weighing more than $2\frac{1}{2}$ tons, but even by the standards of the times it was hardly startling. The steering was particularly light and positive. Indeed, the Phantom III handled better than any previous Rolls-Royce, but it was far from perfect to begin with, as Hives and Robotham discovered when they took a prototype up into the Alps to test the brakes and engine cooling. It must have been a nostalgic journey for Hives, yet the Katschberg Pass was quite unrecognizable from the road that had been the undoing of the 40/50 Ghost in 1912. He and Robotham found that the engine

would not start for 15 minutes after they had stopped to admire the view from the top of the pass. The reason for this was fuel vaporization. When production cars were exported to buyers in Germany a number of engine failures were reported as a result of the cars being driven flat out continuously for hundreds of miles on the newly opened *Autobahnen*. This caused the company to issue a bulletin to owners asking them to restrict continuous cruising speeds to 75–80mph for the Phantom III, 70–75mph for the Phantom II and 65–70mph for the 25/30. Rolls-Royce were criticized for producing cars that could not maintain continuous high speeds, but in fact the company was simply being honest.

The company's testers acknowledged that they had never known a car which was so difficult and time absorbing to work on because of the need to remove components in order to get at others. The four carburettors with which the prototypes were fitted were mainly responsible for this. They had to be very carefully aligned and special spanners were needed to get at the holding-down nuts. The sparking plugs inside the vee of the engine were also inaccessible. In order to remove the sump the exhaust system had to be dismantled, the clutch plate taken off and a juggling act done with the engine. A similar problem arose with the clutch, which took a highly experienced team of mechanics four hours to get at. In all, the first 10,000-mile test produced 34 failures. By the time the car was announced most of the problems had been resolved. The four single carburettors, for example, were replaced by a single, four-choke Stromberg instrument specially made for Rolls-Royce. Spark plug inaccessibility was overcome by putting a special spanner in the tool kit. Although the front suspension initially posed problems with oil seals, bearings and dampers the design was basically sound and gave a better ride than any previous Rolls-Royce.

Some 700 Phantom IIIs were built and it is doubtful whether any one of them made much of a profit for Rolls-Royce. When production ended in 1939 most of the bugs had been discreetly ironed out through a number of modifications. One of these involved substituting solid lifters for the hydraulic tappets and changing the tappet adjustment to the eccentric type used on earlier Phantom models. It acknowledged the fact that the right kind of oil and oil filtration techniques to allow hydraulic tappets to work properly and without undue maintenance did not then exist.

Despite the increasing volume of aero-engine business from the mid-1930s time was found to improve considerably the 20/25 and to introduce a completely new small car, the Wraith. The improved model was the 25/30, introduced in 1936, which marked the ultimate development of the Twenty. Many maintain that it was the nicest small Rolls-Royce of all, and in two years 1,200 were sold to an enthusiastic public. For this car the bore size was given the final stretch from 3.25in to 3.5in which raised capacity to 4,257cc. At the same time the inlet manifolding was

A 1936 25/30 sports limousine by Thrupp and Maberly. The 25/30 marked a further development of the Twenty. It was produced from 1936 until 1938

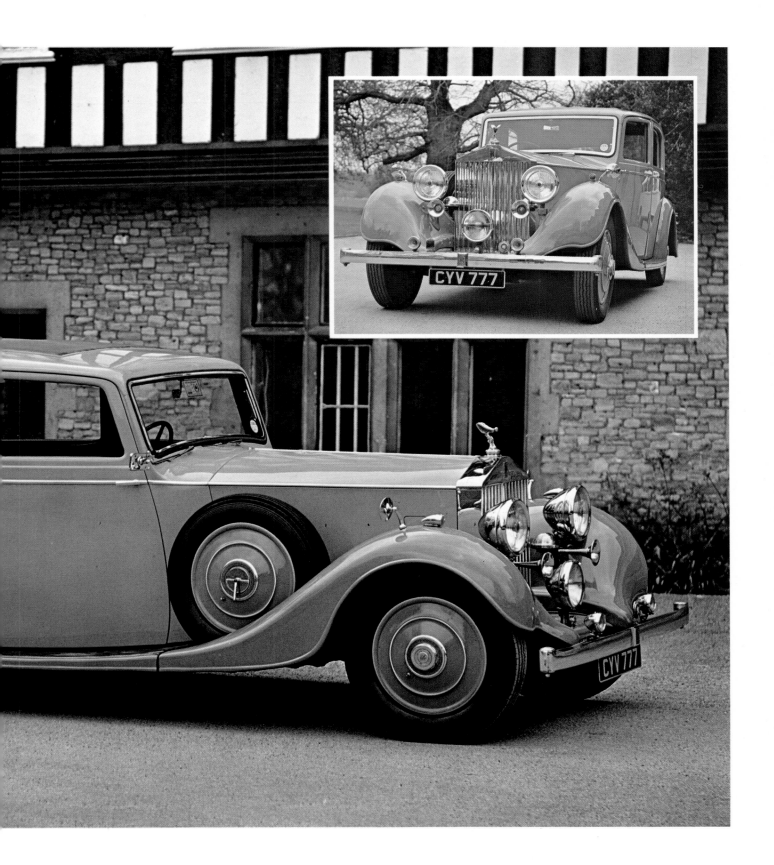

redesigned to bring the carburettor, a down-draught Zenith, to the same side of the engine as the exhaust manifold where it benefited from having a direct hot spot but caused the occasional conflagration. Both the block and the head of the 25/30 were new.

Basically the chassis was the same as that of the 20/25 but it was generally strengthened. The 25/30 perpetuated the controllable hydraulic dampers that had been introduced on the 20/25 in 1934. Wheelbase was increased from 129in to 132in and there was a miniscule increase in track. After the death of Royce proprietary parts were used much more frequently. This trend was fostered by Robotham who rightly believed that the component specialists had the time and resources to develop these items and thereby leave the car manufacturer free to concentrate on areas of more direct concern to him. Thus the 25/30 and later versions of the 20/25 had Marles steering and DWS permanent jacking systems, and the amount of Lucas equipment proliferated with each succeeding model.

Exactly three years after the introduction of the Phantom III its small counterpart, the Wraith, was announced. Many enthusiasts regard the Wraith as the most enjoyable Rolls-Royce of all. Robotham described it disparagingly as a slightly pregnant 25/30. But the Wraith was genuinely exciting and it incorporated fresh and clever ideas. Innovations included a brand new welded chassis frame, which meant the end of tapered bolts. There was a new light-alloy six-cylinder engine with cross-flow head and much improved performance. It was slightly bigger than the 25/30 with a 136in wheelbase, $58\frac{1}{2}$in front and $59\frac{1}{2}$in rear track; it weighed 3,038lb (108lb more than the 25/30) in chassis form.

The new engine had much the same crankcase and bottom end as the 25/30 but the new light-alloy block made use of some Phantom III features, especially the wet liners sealed with rubber rings. The lightweight engine construction compensated for some of the extra weight that had been built into the car to increase the stiffness of the frame and improve road-holding. The extra power to pull this weight came from a new cylinder head. Here

Above and opposite: The Wraith was built in 1938 and 1939. This Park Ward saloon dates from 1939, the year Park Ward was bought by Rolls-Royce

the Bentley inheritance was apparent. Since 1922 Rolls-Royce 20hp series engines had laboured under the disadvantage of having the inlet and exhaust ports on the same side of the engine as the push-rods. Since the head was only 21½in long and 6in of that was taken up by the push-rod tubes there was not much room left for the ports. As mentioned in the preceding chapter all the exhaust ports were siamesed as were two pairs of inlet ports. Now the designers disengaged the inlet ports from the push-rods by putting them on the other side of the engine so that each cylinder could have its own inlet port, which gave improvement in both breathing and power output.

Rolls-Royce were able to produce this very much improved chassis with no increase in price. At £1,100 the Wraith cost in 1938 the same as the less complicated Twenty did 16 years before. It was available with a very pretty four-light, four-door Park Ward touring saloon body for £1,695. Test cars for the press were not available until after the outbreak of war, when the drivers wrote glowingly of the general silence of the car and its

extreme refinement. Reference was made to the silence of the transmission and how easy it was to mistake third gear for top. The synchromesh on second, third and top gears earned high praise and cruising speed was estimated at an effortless 75mph. In its test report *Autocar* remarked that the speedometer recorded 80mph and 84mph on two or three occasions.

The year 1939 marked the end of an era for the company. The old guard of management had almost gone. Arthur Wormald, who had helped Royce build the first Royce car and ultimately became works manager, retired in 1936 and was succeeded by Hives. Elliott was firmly entrenched as chief engineer. Robotham, Hives's lieutenant since 1923, was now head of motor car engineering and was pondering the economics of producing several different chassis with few interchangeable components. Clearly a much different company with a more rational range of cars would emerge at the end of the war that Britain now found herself fighting.

CHAPTER 7

The Coachbuilder's Art

When four head-lamps became fashionable on cars in the 1960s the great Italian automobile designer, Battista Farina, remarked that designing bodies to go with them was rather like designing dresses for women with four breasts. His reference to dresses at least was apt because motor car bodywork is indeed the dress that clothes the chassis; it serves to hide what the designer does not want people to see and emphasizes, temptingly, its attractions. In its long history the basic purpose of coachbuilding has hardly changed.

Coachbuilding was already well developed when the Roman bloods drove their richly decorated chariots through the streets of Ancient Rome. An exquisite Egyptian chariot was found in the tomb of the young king Tutankhamun, and the Greeks had travelled in two- and four-wheeled vehicles, some with enclosed bodies, in their heyday. Because they built good roads the Romans were able to develop the use of wheeled vehicles. They built a wide range of both two-wheeled and four-wheeled carriages and coaches, usually with a great deal of decoration. When the Roman Empire fell, the art of coachbuilding went into decline. The craft did not come into its own again until medieval times, although even then the use of coaches was considered effete and was restricted by law; citizens were encouraged to ride horses instead. It revived, nevertheless, in the regions of present-day Germany, Holland and especially Hungary. Indeed, the word 'coach' is derived from the Hungarian town of Kocs, a coachbuilding centre in medieval times.

The first British-built coach was ordered from Walter Rippon of York in 1555 by the Earl of Rutland. Rippon's first royal order was for Mary Queen of Scots the following year and Elizabeth I ordered a coach shortly afterwards, although it is said that she preferred a Belgian-made conveyance. A number of developments occurred a century later when the leaf-spring was invented, making possible vehicles that were lighter and more comfortable. About that time, too, in 1670, the *Berline* was invented in Berlin. Its significance lies in the fact that it possessed two chassis members instead of the single central pole that had hitherto formed the chassis of carts and coaches. It was thus the true forebear of the motor car chassis frame. In 1677 the Worshipful Company of Coachmakers and Coach Harness Makers was founded in London and from that time British coachbuilding began to take the lead from the French and secured it firmly in the 18th century.

A coachbuilder's establishment in horse-carriage days included several different crafts. There would be blacksmiths to forge the metal fittings and brackets; wheelwrights; joiners to frame the body; panel-workers to fashion the wooden panels; trimmers and upholsterers. Originally the upholsterer who applied the horsehair padding and foundation to the seat was a different tradesman from the trimmer, who covered the seat with materials that ranged from silk to leather. Nowadays the two trades are combined.

Opposite and above: A 1931–32 Phantom II bodied by Park Ward for Mrs Churchill Wylie, a keen traveller. The boot incorporated a washing basin

The Coachbuilder's Art

With the advent of the motor car in the late-19th century the ability to provide a body was already available and the skills of the coachmakers were happily paid for by automobile designers. Only later, when the art of engine and chassis design had become established, did the car-makers find time to devote greater attention to bodies and find new ways of making them. Not surprisingly, therefore, the method of building bodies on early Rolls-Royce cars, and most other makes, differed little from the practice of a century earlier.

The main shape of the body was framed-up in well-seasoned hardwood, usually ash, employing basic joinery techniques, and this was then panelled with wood or metal. In the horse era panels of walnut or mahogany were used exclusively and persisted to a small degree in the motor carriage trade up to the 1920s. The required double curvature was obtained by wetting one side of the wood and heating the other side over a fire. The panels were then quickly pinned to the frame before they lost their shape. Metal panelling, however, is a purely automotive development. It is said to have been started in 1902 by Rothschild et Fils in Belgium when the firm was asked to build a rather curvacious body – a style later known as Roi des Belges – on a Mercedes that the Belgian king had commissioned for his close friend Mlle Cléo de Mérode. From that time onwards the use of aluminium panels on a wooden frame became almost universal practice in high-quality bodywork. Later, steel panels superseded aluminium, especially in the United States where the necessary machines and techniques were developed.

For several decades after the development of the motor car it was the rule rather than the exception for manufacturers of the better cars to offer a chassis only and for the client to have a body built by a coachbuilder. Very often the coachbuilder ordered the chassis. Other motorists might have a body that they were particularly fond of transferred from one car to another. A car could even be provided with more than one body – a two-seater racing style, say, and a four-seater touring body. Quite often buyers of a used car might take a dislike to

the original body and have a new one built. Or the vendors, who were often the manufacturers, would find a certain style of body unsaleable and have the chassis rebodied with a style more in demand. This happened often in America, for example, where records compiled by Rolls-Royce enthusiasts show that some chassis were rebodied two or three times. When sales were sluggish, especially in the Depression, it was quite usual for limousine bodies to be taken off Silver Ghost chassis and replaced by the more attractive roadster style.

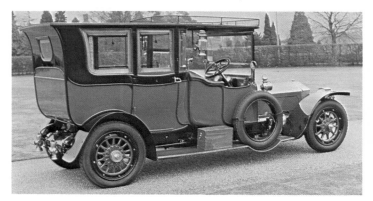

This fine example of Edwardian coachbuilding on a 1911 Silver Ghost chassis was executed by Joseph Lawton of Liverpool. It is a tulip-backed limousine, so-called because of the rear styling. Inset is one of the side-lamps

In both Britain and the United States Rolls-Royce did much for the coachbuilding trade. Henry Royce saw little point in building a fine chassis if it was then provided with a body that was heavy and ill balanced. For this reason Ivan Evernden, one of Royce's most dedicated assistants, maintained close contact with British coachbuilders to make sure that they built bodies to Rolls-Royce standards. By gentle persuasion Evernden helped them to improve their techniques when the bodies broke up in the course of the brutal tests imposed on the chassis at Châteauroux. When limousine and saloon bodies were subjected to these trials in the 1920s the testers screwed the doors shut to prevent them flying open and causing accidents. The men got in and out of the car through the windows; later, when sunshine roofs came into vogue, they could also use the roof. For his personal cars Royce chose simple body-styles and liked them to be compact. He had them painted his own particular shade of grey at a time when funereal black was widely favoured for cars of the Rolls-Royce type.

The first fundamental change in body construction in Europe came in the mid-1920s with the Weymann body. Born in Haiti and brought up in France, Charles Terres Weymann gained considerable fame as a pioneer aviator, taking second place in the first Schneider Trophy race in 1913, before turning his attention to motor cars. He opened premises in the Rue Troyon in Paris, where he sold car bodies and motoring accessories. All chassis of this period flexed and wracked even on smooth roads and Weymann sought to rectify this. Instead of building bodies that resisted the stresses imposed by bumpy road surfaces he evolved a method of construction that produced a body that could 'ride' with the roughness. Weymann's car bodies were framed-up in ash in the normal way, but instead of connecting the timbers by woodworkers' joints he joined them with flexible metal brackets that did not allow adjoining pieces of wood to touch. Oiled felt was usually interposed between the joint as an additional safeguard. This system did away with the creaking and groaning at the joints to which even the best traditionally built bodies were prone after a short time. And Weymann's bodies were not panelled in metal; they were covered, instead, with imitation leather-cloth or leather stretched over horsehair padding. Where double curves were required the padding was supported by expanded light-metal panels tacked to the framing. These bodies were silent and also very light, which helped the performance of the car. For these reasons they enjoyed a considerable vogue and licences to build them were granted to many of the great coachbuilders of the time. In Britain a Weymann Motor Body Company was formed.

One further reason for the popularity of the Weymann type of construction was that, at a time when car production was rising fast, it overcame the problem, increasingly difficult, of finding sufficient skilled panel-beaters; and so mass-produced, imitation Weymann bodies began to appear. These suffered from most of the disadvantages of the construction methods while displaying few of the advantages. Moreover, they were built from second-class materials and if left out in the weather they quickly rotted. This brought the method undeservedly into disrepute. A valid complaint, however, concerned the surface finish of the leather-cloth or leather, which was dull. Attempts were made to counteract this by panelling the bodies up to the waistline, but they were unsuccessful because the end result was a body half-rigid and half-flexible and which inevitably developed rattles. Very fine Weymann bodies were built on Rolls-Royce chassis by coachbuilders such as H. J. Mulliner, Vanden Plas, Gurney Nutting and others.

As far as Europe went, the next most important step in car-body construction was the advent of the pressed-steel body. That development had already occurred in America where individual pressed panels had been used long before the First World War and where, in 1913, Edward G. Budd had persuaded John and Horace Dodge to let him design and tool an all-pressed-steel body. Budd's other achievements included a stainless-steel rail-coach and the Ford Trimotor aeroplane.

William Morris, later Lord Nuffield, introduced the pressed-steel body to England in 1926 when, with the help of Budd's company

The interior of this 1927 Phantom I by Clark of Wolverhampton imitates Louis XIV style. The division conceals extra seats; the sofa is worked in Aubusson petit point, and the ceiling was painted in France

and the bankers J. H. Schroeder, he founded the Pressed Steel Company in Oxford. It brought the advantage of rapid production and the drawback of inflexibility which came from high-volume output. Those early pressed bodies were not the unitary structures we know today. They were simply bodies of the old type ready to mount on separate chassis and they differed only in that they were made from steel pressings welded together. Exposed joints were 'joggled' and then filled with lead to give a smooth surface. They still contained a quantity of wood, mainly for door cappings and for the tacking strips to which the body interior trim was fastened. Initially the entire production of the Pressed Steel Company was reserved for Morris Motors but later on the company took orders from other popular makes.

Prior to 1939 in Europe steel bodies were reserved for the lower end of the market. Firms such as Rolls-Royce, Daimler, Lanchester and Bentley continued to patronize the traditional coachbuilders and traditional methods of coachbuilding. Europe took a jump ahead of the United States when Citroen in 1934 introduced the *traction avant* with the body and chassis in one unit. Rolls-Royce did not adopt steel construction until 1946.

Gurney Nutting mounted this fixed head coupe on a 1933 Phantom II Continental. It is considered one of the most desirable of all body-styles

The main reason the company switched to steel then was similar to that which prompted the Dodge brothers in 1913 and William Morris in 1926 – insufficient craftsmen were available to build bodies in the required quantities.

By moving over to pressed-steel bodywork Rolls-Royce found it necessary to accept the restrictions that the big tooling investment in a steel body places on the ability to make frequent design changes. The relatively low volume of Rolls-Royce and Bentley production meant that die costs had to be amortized over a long period. The company also had to accept the fact that a steel body, unless very well protected, enjoyed a life no longer than that of a Weymann body because of the natural tendency of steel to revert to iron oxide. In the early days of steel-body production at Crewe the steel sheet available in postwar Britain was not always of best quality. Moreover, the designers had not fully appreciated the need to eliminate water traps and to ensure that all sill areas were fully ventilated. Many owners found that the car body decayed long before the chassis parts were anywhere near the end of their life. On the latest cars these problems have been overcome but the first 10 years of steel-body production often proved troublesome for the company.

Many fine enclosed bodies were built on Rolls-Royce chassis during the Edwardian era but the majority of the bodies mounted on the early chassis were open styles with and without windscreens. The small windscreen was slow to evolve. Early ones tended to be almost the size of a small shop-window. Made of glass they were heavy and unsightly. Many enclosed bodies did not have windscreens; the driver sat in the open air perhaps under the shelter of an extension of the enclosed rear compartment. The feature that most dated the cars built before the First World War was the low radiator and bonnet line. These components of early Rolls-Royce cars, up to the 1912 and 1913 Silver Ghosts, were long, low and level. The bonnets had parallel sides and butted up against a flat dash. Possibly Napier started the trend to higher radiators – they moved theirs forward at the same time – and brought the top of the bonnet more or less in line with the waist of the car. The London-Edinburgh Rolls-Royce was the first model of the marque to have a tall radiator and a tapered scuttle rather than a flat one. This change revolutionized the appearance of the car despite the fact that little was altered behind the windscreen. The tourer bodies built for the Austrian Alpine Trial cars – called the Continental by Claude Johnson and the Alpine Eagle by Ernest Hives – were among the most handsome put on any car before 1914. They served as a model for Rolls-Royce touring styles for many years after the war in common with the chassis they were mounted on.

When Hives visited America in 1922 he received a favourable impression of American custom coachwork. Rolls-Royce engineers had always chafed at the conservative methods of British coachbuilders and Hives found the American approach refreshing. Materials were of high quality and the standard of workmanship first-rate. Bodies with clean lines emerged from American coachbuilding companies. The Salamanca town car was a classic formal car. The Piccadilly roadster and the Stratford coupe, with their severe, pure waistlines, contrasted markedly with a few broken-backed productions that were built by one or two British coachbuilders during the production life of the 40/50hp Ghost. Of the many different bodies mounted on English Rolls-Royce chassis by the principal coachbuilders not a few have become classics. One is the barrel-bodied Barker tourer, so-called because of the bulbous section of the side panels. Another in the same class is the enclosed cabriolet, also by Barker, on the Ghost and New Phantom chassis.

With the launch of the Phantom II, and the trend for close-coupled coachwork, the spare wheels were moved from the running-boards to the back which gave the body designers greater scope for invention. The standard close-coupled saloon with flared wings, devised by Ivan Evernden in conjunction with Barker, has attained classic status, as has the Park Ward coupe on the Continental chassis and Hooper's Phantom II sedanca de ville. Some very beautiful convertible bodies were put on

One man's taste. Mr Nubar Gulbenkian ordered this sedanca, a startling departure from tradition, for a Silver Wraith chassis. It was built by Hooper

Opposite top: A colour drawing by a Hooper artist of a Silver Wraith touring saloon
Opposite centre: A 1952 catalogue picture of a Silver Wraith touring limousine by Hooper
Opposite: Front seats of a 1967 Silver Shadow

Phantom II Continental chassis. Barker did a first-class one, so did Park Ward and Gurney Nutting. When the Phantom III appeared with its very high waistline the stylists handled it just as well. There were quite a number of really memorable bodies mounted on the Phantom III chassis, and excellent work was being done on Bentleys at the same time. James Young produced a Phantom III sports saloon body that was widely copied.

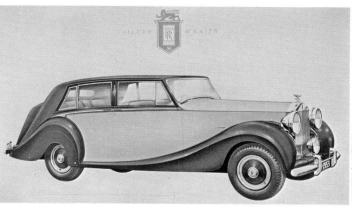

By 1945 the number of coachbuilders in Britain had shrunk dramatically. The survivers were H. J. Mulliner, Park Ward (since 1939 owned by Rolls-Royce), James Young of Bromley, and several smaller concerns. Although Rolls-Royce now made their own steel bodies, chassis only were still available and this allowed the company to reintroduce the Continental (with a Bentley radiator), a very handsome prototype saloon by Pininfarina on the Silver Dawn chassis. Although the Phantom V chassis was intended for formal coachwork there was no reason why it could not receive owner-driver bodies, but no one seems to have responded to the challenge. The Silver Shadow, because of its unitary construction, comes now in standard bodies but for those who want something different from the standard four-door saloon there is the Corniche, in open or enclosed form, and the Pininfarina-styled Camargue, the first Rolls-Royce to go into production with bodywork from this eminent Italian stylist.

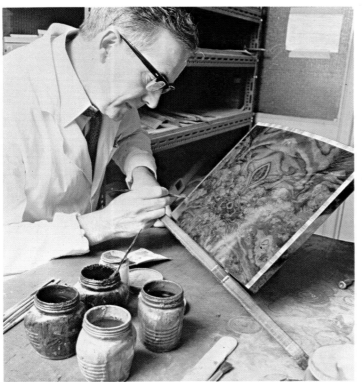

Having done so much to keep traditional coachbuilders in business between the wars it is fitting that Rolls-Royce should now own what is probably the largest custom coachbuilder in the world. This is Mulliner Park Ward, with workshops at Willesden and Harlesden in London. H. J. Mulliner had been acquired in the late 1950s and in 1961 was merged with Park Ward to form the Rolls-Royce coachbuilding division. At Mulliner Park Ward and at James Young in Bromley (still active as coachwork restorers) one can see old-fashioned craftsmanship being used to frame-up bodies (in well-seasoned ash until recently) and panel-beaters forming the panels from sheets of aluminium to skin the body.

Until recently a drawing was always made of the proposed body. It was what the coachbuilders called a 'picture' – a side elevation and possibly a rear view, usually coloured for the client. From this and a few simple dimensions the foreman coachbuilder supervised the framing of the body, often drawing units full size on the floor in chalk. The panel-beaters then skinned the body, beating out the double curvature of the panels on wooden blocks and leather bags filled with sand or lead-shot. Before the advent of wheeling machines, hammer marks were filed out and later, if they were too deep, filled with stopping when the body was being painted. Wheeling machines, which consist of a large cast-iron frame supporting two steel, doughnut-shaped wheels of different radii and adjustable camber, have revolutionized bespoke body manufacture. Two

Top: A French polisher colours
veneer in order to emphasize
both pattern and shade
Above: A Phantom VI landaulet
limousine built in 1974

men working as a team operate them to produce double curvature panels which look as though they have come from a press. Panel-beating is as much an art as a craft and good men are worth every penny they earn.

One essentially British speciality is the use of walnut veneers on instrument panels and door cappings. Veneered instrument panels are a feature of every Rolls-Royce car be it steel-bodied or custom made and they are manufactured by the old process of cutting and glueing the veneers onto a stable wooden base, staining them selectively to bring out the best of the grain, and then finishing them with many coats of varnish. It is a measure of Rolls-Royce thoroughness that a sample of the veneer from every car is carefully filed for future reference.

Coach-painting has undergone many changes since the days when oil-based paints and varnishes were applied by brush. As many as 20 coats were applied, with hand flatting between in top-quality work. Final varnishing was a highly particular skill. It could only be done when the weather conditions were right and then only the best man in the shop was entrusted with the task. During the enormous expansion of production in the 1920s the Americans had to find an alternative to multiple coats and brush painting because of the shortage of workmen skilled in the job. Cellulose provided the answer, but effectively only from 1926 and the invention of the spray-gun. From then on cellulose was used for all except very special work until the introduction of special paints, such as acrylics, and low-bake ovens came into use after 1945.

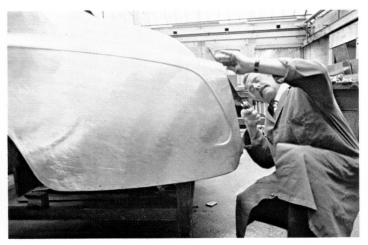

Above: Interior of the 1974 Phantom VI illustrated opposite, showing TV set, drinks compartment, radio controls and foldaway seats

Three panel-beaters at work at the Mulliner Park Ward Division of Rolls-Royce in London: working on the body (top), beating out the rear window surround (centre) and shaping a rear wing (above)

124

CHAPTER 8

The Continuing Tradition

Rolls-Royce emerged from the Second World War riding high. Their Merlin engines had powered the Spitfires and Hurricanes that won the Battle of Britain and they had been the motive power for the Lancasters and Mosquitos which pounded Germany by night. Even the American Army Fortresses which bombed Germany by day were protected by Merlin-engined Mustangs on their long forays over eastern Germany and Berlin. Never would Ernest Hives allow the car business to jeopardize Rolls-Royce pre-eminence in aero-engine manufacture, yet there was never any intention of letting car production stop. Hives believed that the aero-engine side should not subsidize car production, as it had done before the war. He realized that the expensive cars that Derby had built before 1939 could not be a profitable undertaking in postwar economic conditions and he was determined that the company should rid itself of what he called 'the Phantom III complex'. The possibility of setting up

a separate car division was considered at one point and it was decided that after the war car work should be moved to Crewe. Meanwhile, all work to do with wheeled or track-laying vehicles had been transferred to the Clan works at Belper, where W. A. Robotham had done sterling work converting the Merlin aero-engine into the Meteor tank engine and virtually designing the Cromwell tank to put it in.

As the war drew to a close a number of prototypes were designed at Belper. Probably the most interesting was a car, codenamed Myth, that had an engine small enough to go into the current Austin Eight, which it imbued with a top speed of 76mph. When it got into the Rolls-Royce chassis intended for it, however, the in-built weight factor reduced performance dramatically. As the company found yet again, it cost almost as much to make a small car as it does a big car. The project was dropped.

Opposite: The Camargue was introduced in 1975. It is a two-door saloon
Above: A 1954 Silver Wraith limousine by Hooper

A successor to the Phantom III type of vehicle, codenamed Big Bertha, was more significant. It was powered by a straight-eight F-head engine that had been undergoing development since 1935 when a newcomer to the design department, Jack Phillips, started running a single-cylinder test engine of this configuration. The idea was to develop a series of engines of four, six and eight cylinders all sharing the same components. Codenamed the B-series, these engines were originally conceived as car units but were also destined to achieve fame as motive power for military vehicles. They were very much Robotham's concern, and he had one of the eight-cylinder units squeezed into a Bentley chassis.

This device, nicknamed Scalded Cat, was by all accounts trouble-free and had so much performance that most of the testers at Derby frightened themselves with it at some time or another. But none of them succeeded in writing it off. Robotham used the car regularly for commuting and liked it so much that he proposed it to Jack Barclay as a basis for the postwar Bentley. Barclay, concerned about the potential mortality rate among his clientele, thought otherwise. Scalded Cat was kept on the fleet until one day, when the Phantom IV was under way, the Duke of Edinburgh requested the loan of it. The car was returned intact, but mindful that the same request might be made again the company scrapped the car in the interests of prudence. Another project, the Rippletto, which was intended as a replacement for the 25/30, used a four-cylinder B-series engine but it was abandoned because of the persistent occurrence of engine-mounting problems.

Before the war, combined Rolls-Royce and Bentley production had been around 1,500 cars a year. All these chassis required specialized coachwork. When the war ended many of the companies that had built bodies had vanished. Their skilled workforces had been dispersed – many moved into the aircraft industry – or just retired. What remained of the British coach-building industry in 1945 was certainly not sufficient to cope with 1,500 chassis per year let alone the larger volume that Rolls-Royce planned.

Clearly, the company would have to make their own bodies, and they would have to be made from pressed steel. When Hives had made his swap of the Meteor tank engine for the Rover company's pioneering axial-flow jet engine, Robotham had become friendly with Spencer Wilks, the founder of the Rover company as we know it today, and consulted him about making high-quality pressed bodies. As a consequence Ivan Evernden produced some ideas of what kind of body was likely to be wanted and in January 1944 discussions began with the Pressed Steel Company in Oxford. Despite initial alarm at the prospect of spending £250,000 on a set of body tools the project was approved and a body-design section established at Belper.

The Silver Dawn, produced at first for export only, became available in Britain in 1953, the year this saloon was built. It was the first model to carry a steel production (as opposed to a coachbuilt) body

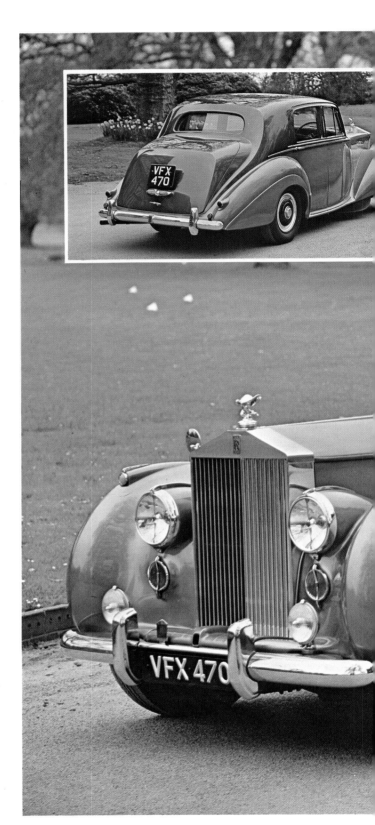

*Top: This 1956 Silver Wraith
touring limousine was bodied by
H. J. Mulliner
Above: A 1955 Silver Cloud I
four-door saloon*

During the latter part of 1945 the Crewe factory was turned over to motor car manufacture with Dr Llewellyn Smith as managing director. The technical press were able to drive the first postwar Rolls-Royce in April 1946, and the first car bodied by Pressed Steel was seen the same year behind a Bentley radiator. Both these cars, the Silver Wraith and the Bentley Mk VI, had many components in common. Apart from the chassis length and the fact that the Silver Wraith had a single Stromberg carburettor and the Bentley twin SUs and different gear ratios, they were almost identical.

The Silver Wraith at this stage followed Rolls-Royce tradition in being offered on a chassis-only basis but the Bentley from the start was sold with the pressed-steel body designed at Belper, although it could, of course, be bought as a chassis only. The B-series engine that powered these cars was destined to be the motive unit for Rolls-Royce and Bentley cars for the next 13 years. As already mentioned, work was begun in 1935 on an F-head, an engine with the inlet valve in the head and the exhaust valve at the side in the block. This work started because the Rolls-Royce foundry was finding it difficult to cast heads for the small six-cylinder models with predictable water space around the in-line valves. A major problem with the 20/25 engine had been a tendency for cracks to form between the valve seats. By putting the inlet valve in the head and the exhaust valve in the block this problem was overcome and it was possible to provide plenty of water space round the exhaust and inlet valves and at the same time achieve a more efficient combustion chamber. The advantages gained proved to be considerable.

The cylinder dimensions of this new Rolls-Royce engine were $3\frac{1}{2}$in × $4\frac{1}{2}$in to give a cubic swept volume of 4,257cc. Harry Grylls, who succeeded Robotham as chief engineer of the car division, has written a most interesting paper on the development of the 20hp series of engines, of which the Silver Wraith unit was one, pointing out how the size of the cylinder centres, namely 4.15in, remained unchanged from 1922 to 1959, when the V8 engine was introduced. (It is worth pointing out here the equally fascinating fact that from the introduction of the 40/50 Silver Ghost in 1907 until 1959 the stroke of every Rolls-Royce engine was $4\frac{1}{2}$in, with the exception of the Phantom I and II, which suggests that the company got very good value from their crankshaft turning fixtures.) The cylinder head of this new engine was an RR50 aluminium alloy casting with inserted valve seats while the combined cylinder block and upper half of the crankcase were cast iron. A not entirely successful innovation, however, was to chromium-plate the upper section of the cylinder bores, where most bore-wear occurs. Problems associated with this arrangement were resolved later in the life of the engine. They were overcome by inserting a special iron liner at this point.

During the war enormous advances had been made in the development of materials, and the new cars had hardened steel crankshafts and lead-bronze bearings. The crankshaft itself followed Rolls-Royce practice, having hollow journals throughout with the usual closing plates. The latest type of slipper flywheel was fitted in company with the thin, spring-diaphragm flywheel that had been found to eliminate flywheel thunder. Many features of the engine were not only rationalized but more rational. In the days before the invention of reliable V-belts Henry Royce's preference for all-gear drives for the ancillaries was logical enough. In 1946 this was no longer necessary, and a single belt sufficed to drive the water pump, fan and dynamo of the Silver Wraith engine. The distributor was driven in the universally accepted manner by a skew gear in the middle of the camshaft. The cost-saving in this area of the engine must have been considerable, but tradition lingered on in the shape of the specially built starter with reduction gear to ensure silent operation. Dual ignition had now gone for ever and the carburettor, a dual-choke, downdraught Stromberg on a water-heated manifold, may have been specially made for Rolls-Royce but near cousins were to be found on much less prestigious makes. For the first time Rolls-Royce Limited mentioned horsepower figures (something they had previously avoided) and revealed that the new engine gave 137bhp at 4,400rpm with an open exhaust on the test bed and about 122bhp when installed.

Laying out the chassis, the Belper team had resisted the temptation to reproduce the pre-war Wraith chassis and had designed a relatively simple, parallel girder frame upswept over the back axle and with an enormous cruciform member stretching from the top of the rear wheel arches to the rear engine mountings to resist torsional stresses and more than compensate for the boxed side-members of the old Wraith. There was also a new type of independent front suspension with the lower links extended to the middle of the chassis and pivoting on rubber bushes. They were braced by forged radius arms picking up with brackets on the side-members so that, in effect, the triangle thus formed acted as a leading link in contrast with the trailing link geometry of pre-war Phantom IIIs and Wraiths. The relatively short upper suspension link pivoted on the spindle of the front shock-absorbers and was angled forward to fit in with the geometry of the lower triangle. The object of this exercise was to reduce nose-dive effect on braking. The suspension medium was vertical coil springs at the front and long, gaitered springs at the back. Tradition was perpetuated in the well engineered synchromesh gearbox with right-hand change and the traditional gearbox-driven brake servo which now actuated the front brakes hydraulically. Henry Royce would have approved of this, but possibly not the pull-on handbrake with its attendant cable.

This basic chassis and engine combination served the company well until 1955. In that time the engine bore size was progressively increased to $3\frac{5}{8}$in in 1951 to bring capacity up to 4,566cc and in 1955 to $3\frac{3}{4}$in, taking the size up to 4,887cc. Many minor modifications resulted from experience. One of these involved replacing the fabric-plastic composition camshaft gear with an aluminium one in 1950, because drivers on the Continent could maintain high speeds long enough to raise oil temperatures to the point where the composition gear began to disintegrate. Bentley drivers discovered this, predictably; it was on them that Rolls-Royce owners depended for most technical developments.

A Rolls-Royce motor car with the standard steel body did not appear until 1949, when the Silver Dawn was announced. This was virtually a Mk VI Bentley with a Rolls-Royce radiator and a Stromberg carburettor to give improved low-speed tractability at the expense of top speed. It was on the same 120in-wheelbase Bentley chassis and was offered originally for export only to satisfy the United States market. The Silver Dawn did not come on the British market until 1953, by which time it had acquired the larger and better-looking luggage boot that distinguished the R-type Bentley. By then English buyers had the benefit of the $3\frac{5}{8}$in bore engine. The price of the standard saloon in 1953 was £4,605.

Above: A Silver Cloud I saloon from 1956
Opposite top: A 1957 drop head coupe
Silver Cloud I by H. J. Mulliner
Opposite: Hooper mounted this limousine
on a 1957 Silver Wraith chassis

A year prior to the introduction of the Silver Dawn a significant step forward was taken with the adoption of automatic transmission as an alternative to the Rolls-Royce synchromesh box. The main elements of automatic transmission were not new. The principle of the torque convertor had been laid down before 1900, Henry Ford used an epicyclic gearbox on the immortal Model T, and Major Wilson had developed a four-speed epicyclic gearbox for use in tanks during the First World War. It took the English Daimler company to put a fluid coupling (not a torque convertor) and a Wilson epicyclic gearbox together to make their fluid flywheel and preselector transmission in the early 1930s.

The possibilities of this ingenious marriage were largely ignored in Britain. But they did not escape the attention of General Motors engineers. During the pre-war period, GM developed a refined and fully automatic gearbox using basically the same fluid coupling and epicyclic gear elements of the Daimler transmission but in which the gear shifts took place automatically in response to signals from the accelerator position and car speed. Furthermore, they added the refinement of a mechanical override control that allowed the driver to select any gear he wanted if he did not agree with what the gearbox thought. This Hydramatic transmission was first fitted to Oldsmobile cars in 1938 and was just one of a number of

automatic transmissions developed in the United States at that time. In the war it found application on military vehicles and by the end of hostilities had proved itself. Its obvious possibilities had not escaped Rolls-Royce, whose admiration for the expertise of General Motors caused them to keep a close eye on what the corporation was doing. It was exactly what they wanted because it was a four-step unit – all the other American transmissions had three steps, or even two – and it gave their customers, who included many experienced and discerning drivers, the chance to make their own decision about gear shifting if they desired to do so.

Soon after the war Robotham travelled to the United States and negotiated a manufacturing agreement with GM whose president, Charles Wilson, found it difficult to understand why the British should wish to make this complicated unit at the rate of 5,000 units a year – the figure quoted by Robotham, although in reality it turned out to be less than half this figure – when they could buy it from America off the shelf. Rolls-Royce wanted to make it to their own standards, however, and needed to incorporate their gearbox-driven servo. A licensing agreement was finalized and Rolls-Royce-built Hydramatics were offered to members of the motoring public at the 1952 motor show in London.

The period 1950 to 1953 was a time of change in the design team at Rolls-Royce. During the Belper period Robotham had developed a line of successful diesel engines that were finding increasing acceptance. At the same time the military versions of the B-series engine, which were of the same configuration as the car engines used in Bentley and Rolls-Royce chassis but had cast-iron heads and other variations, were beginning to be big business too. Accordingly, responsibilities were split. Robotham was given the diesel division to look after, with new offices and works at Derby, while Harry Grylls became chief engineer of the car division with his own design office at Crewe. The military engines were also moved to Crewe with Jack Phillips, who had taken over from Charles Jenner as 'engine man'. Phillips was destined to be responsible for forward design on Rolls-Royce car engines as well.

This team was responsible for the next major change to the Rolls-Royce line in the shape of the Silver Cloud, announced in April 1955. The new model was powered by the B-series six-cylinder unit, now at full stretch, with its bores placed so close together that it was impossible to run the cooling water between them. The rest of the chassis and body were entirely new.

The most obvious changes were that automatic transmission was now standard and the front suspension reverted to the old, Olley-inspired, semi-trailing geometry but was much simplified with vertical coil springs. At the rear end the upsweep over the

axle was taken so close to the wheels that the rear springs had to be set inside the chassis frame instead of outside it. The loss of spring-base with this arrangement, combined with the soft springs called for by the salesmen, caused an unacceptable amount of axle wind-up, which had to be allayed by the use of an ingenious Z-bar mounted on the right-hand side-member. This not only put extra roll stiffness into the rear suspension but also acted as a radius bar to take accelerating and braking forces out of the springs.

Changes to the power train also included a new six-port head – previous engines had four-port heads with the inner pairs of ports siamesed – and a pair of SU carburettors replaced the former two-stroke Stromberg instrument. The carburettors were mounted on a new inlet manifold which was half-formed in the head, the other half being in the shape of a detachable cover. This made it easy to control accurately the inside shape of the

Top: A 1956 Silver Cloud I saloon
Above: This four-door Silver
Cloud I saloon dates from 1959,
the final year of production

manifold. Production of the four-speed, synchromesh gearbox ceased and the Rolls-Royce-built Hydramatic gearbox became standard equipment. The brakes were still operated by mechanical servo although this had been modified to run at a higher speed to eliminate some of the idiosyncracies of the system. Actuation to the back wheels was now hydraulic and brake balance was biased more to the front. Because of a change from 16in to 15in road wheels the brake drums had to be reduced in diameter and therefore were made wider in order to compensate.

It is difficult to ignore the influence of the Park Ward R-type Continental Bentley on the shape of the Silver Cloud body. With its long, sweeping wing-line terminating at just the right point on the shoulder of the rear wings it was arguably the best-looking standard body that had ever been mounted on a Rolls-Royce. Apart from its handsome shape it offered increased interior space, a bigger boot and a proper fresh-air heating system comprehensively arranged to provide fresh or heated air to passengers. The Silver Cloud seemed to be remarkably good value at £4,669. This was only £64 more expensive than the Silver Dawn, yet the new model had a much more comprehensive specification.

The Cloud was offered in two wheelbase lengths, 123in and 127in, with Rolls-Royce bodies. In addition, James Young offered a saloon on the standard chassis and there was a saloon and a limousine by Hooper as well as an extremely handsome drop-head coupe by H. J. Mulliner, soon to be acquired by Rolls-Royce. For those who wanted to buy a Rolls in the old tradition the long wheelbase (133in) Silver Wraith chassis continued in production and was offered with a variety of bodies by Park Ward, H. J. Mulliner, Hooper and James Young.

A 1958 Silver Cloud I four-door saloon. Production of this model, introduced in 1955, exceeded 2,300

There followed a subsequent version of the Silver Cloud which appeared in 1957 when a persistent demand from the American distributors caused power-steering and air conditioning to be added to the specification. In this first installation the evaporator unit was located in the boot underneath the rear parcel shelf and expelled cold air through a grille in the shelf and out of ducts built into the cantrails. The extra power demand from the air conditioning was met by increasing the engine compression ratio from 7.25 : 1 to 8 : 1 on all cars exported to the United States and Canada. This was later to become standard for all Silver Cloud models.

The demand for more and more power for the lucrative American market was eventually met in 1959 when Crewe announced their $6\frac{1}{4}$-litre V8 engine for the Silver Cloud II and the Phantom V, successor to the Silver Wraith. Concurrently with this change the air conditioning system was increased in capacity and the evaporator unit moved into the right-hand front wing to give more boot space.

As soon as the V8 power unit was announced the allegation was made that it merely copied an American unit (Chrysler's was most frequently mentioned). Yet nothing was further from the truth. Admittedly the eight cylinders were arranged in blocks of four set at 90 degrees, but so were those of the Legalimit more than 50 years previously. And if certain American companies were using light-alloy cylinder blocks what about the Merlin engine or the Phantom III of 1935? In fact the choice of a V8 was logical and inevitable in a car the size of the Silver Cloud. It would have been impossible to increase the capacity of the six-cylinder unit without making it very much longer, which would have required a new chassis. A V12 would have been unnecessarily complicated for negligible gain in smoothness. The designers succeeded in avoiding most of the pitfalls of the 12-cylinder Phantom III unit yet reaped the benefit of the latest developments in engine design and combined them with Rolls-Royce experience with light-alloy V-engines gained with the Merlin.

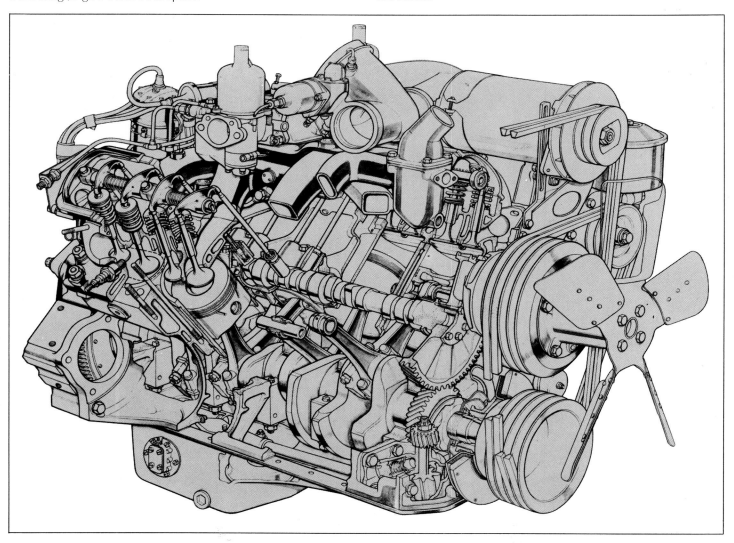

It was certainly a no-nonsense engine with plenty of room for stretch. It was based on a light-alloy block and crankcase casting with inserted wet liners. These liners were sealed in the traditional Rolls-Royce way by rubber ring seals, one at the top of each liner and two around the skirt; as with the Phantom III the area between the two lower seals was vented to atmosphere. Wartime improvements in materials and the advent of Vandervell lead-indium flashed bearings made the Phantom's complex connecting rod arrangement obsolete, so the connecting rods of opposing cylinders ran side-by-side on common crankpins. The connecting rods and crankshaft were, as ever, steel forgings but the oil feeds to the little-end bearings were no longer to be found, and for the first time in the company's history a Rolls-Royce had a solid crankshaft without the traditional hollow journals.

The camshaft, lying in the cleavage of the block, was driven by a forged light-alloy half-time wheel and operated the in-line valves through hydraulic tappets and rockers. These tappets,

Opposite: The 6¼-litre V8 engine was introduced in 1959 on the Silver Cloud II and Phantom V

Top: Dashboard of a 1961 Silver Cloud II limousine by James Young
Above: A 1960 Silver Cloud II saloon

essential in a light-alloy engine because of block expansion, were made under licence from Chrysler, which prompted some to believe that the engine design stemmed from that company. The cylinder heads were, naturally, aluminium with inserted valve seats and the crankcase, which was extended below crankshaft level in the interests of rigidity, was closed by a pressed-steel sump.

Mixture was supplied to the cylinders by two horizontal SU carburettors mounted on a two-tier water-heated manifold. Observers commented that the carburettors and manifolds appeared to be artificially restricted to keep output down to 200bhp. If that was so, the engine had great potential because, with its short, 3.6in stroke, it was capable of running up to 5,000rpm without inciting undue piston speeds. The choice of this relatively short stroke in combination with a 4.1in bore was conditioned by the desire to keep the width of the engine down

Top: Rear of a 1961 Silver Cloud II by James Young. Production lasted from 1959 until 1962

Above: A Silver Cloud III drop head coupe built in 1964 and bodied by Park Ward

and to retain the option of increasing valve sizes without running into the problems that had been experienced in the later stages of 20hp development. One disadvantage was that the choice of pentroof combustion chambers made it necessary to locate the sparking plugs underneath the exhaust manifold. When the engine eventually appeared in the Silver Cloud consternation reigned among purists because owners now had to remove the front wheels and a couple of underwing panels to get at the plugs. But modern sparking plugs did not need to be changed as often as in the past.

The ultimate development of the Silver Cloud was the series III model. This was fundamentally the same as the series II but had a four head-lamp system, causing yet more dismay among traditionalists, and a lowered radiator that brought the appearance into line with contemporary trends and saw the model through to the most revolutionary Rolls-Royce of all, the Silver Shadow.

Top: H. J. Mulliner bodied this Silver Cloud III convertible which dates from 1962

The Phantom IV and Phantom V, meanwhile, although conceived with different objects in mind, were complementary to each other in a way. The Phantom IV was the most exclusive Rolls-Royce of all; it was specifically intended for royalty and heads of state. The first of this series was delivered in 1950 to Princess Elizabeth and her husband, the Duke of Edinburgh. Although members of the British Royal family had owned Rolls-Royces since the mid-1920s this was the first time that a completely new model had been designed especially for members of the British Royal House. The conception of the car and the manner in which it was executed reflected the pleasure and pride that the company felt in the assignment. The Phantom IV is the largest Rolls-Royce yet made, its wheelbase being 1in longer than that of the Phantom V, and the car was also a little heavier. The overall length of the Royal Phantom IV was 228in and its height more than 72in, which caused it to tower over most cars on the road.

Mechanically the main interest in this car was the use of an eight-cylinder B-series engine as the propulsive unit. With a capacity of 5,675cc it had virtually the same engine that the duke had tried out in the Scalded Cat at the time the Phantom IV was being built. The chassis it was installed in was fundamentally the same as that of the Wraith but lengthened to accommodate the longer engine at the front and the more capacious bodywork at the back. Among the many interesting features of this car, which was trimmed and fitted out in the most luxurious manner, but with typical restraint, was its special mascot of St George and the Dragon. Since the first order fewer than 20 Phantom IV cars have been made. Most prospective owners of large Rolls-Royces would need to concentrate their attention on the Phantom V, which replaced the Silver Wraith, and the Phantom VI. Both the Phantom V and Phantom VI have the 6,230cc V8 engine because it is mated with the four-speed Rolls-Royce-GM Hydramatic gearbox which is the only Rolls-Royce transmission having the gearbox-driven servo necessary to operate drum brakes. The main difference between the Phantom V and Phantom VI is that the later model has two separate air-conditioning systems, one for the front compartment and one for the back. In 1979 the Mk VI became available with the 6,750cc engine, three-speed GM400 gearbox and drum brakes operated by a Shadow-type power hydraulic system. These Phantom VIs are claimed to be the best cars in the world and are probably the most expensive, costing around £100,000 each.

Some 60 years after Henry Royce created the 40/50 Ghost, a car which with justification could be claimed to have exceeded all others in excellence, the Crewe design team astonished the motoring world with the Silver Shadow, the most innovatory model that Rolls-Royce had ever produced. On many points it departed from Rolls-Royce engineering practice yet did not abandon principles. For one thing it was of monocoque construction with the front and rear suspensions carried on separate subframes, the front one also supporting the engine. The suspension was automatically adjusted for height by a power hydraulic system that also provided power to operate the brakes and did away with the gearbox-driven servo. There was also a new, recirculating ball steering gear with integral power assistance, an electrically operated gearshift and electrically operated window lifts and seat adjustment. All these new features were refined to a high degree by customary Rolls-Royce rig-testing.

Probably the most revolutionary feature of the Silver Shadow was the power hydraulic system, operating at a pressure of 2,500psi, which derived from a pair of small plunger pumps that worked off the engine camshaft. Pressure was stored in spherical accumulators made under Citroen patents with butyl separators and nitrogen 'springs'. Pressure from these accumulators operated hydraulic rams in the rear suspension to jack up the springs within a range of 3in; the front suspension could be varied within a range of 1in. The height was automatically adjusted according to the load when the car was on the move or, if it was stationary, when the doors were opened or the gear lever put into neutral.

The power system operated the brakes which were, in effect, divided into three separate systems, four if the handbrake is included. Two of these, the front and the rear, were operated through the medium of a Citroen-type pedal valve. Since the Crewe engineers did not feel that the rather abrupt action of that valve would suit their customers they did not operate it directly but introduced a third, hydrostatic, circuit. This operated one of the two sets of pads in the rear brakes and activated the Citroen valve by pressure, thereby giving the brake pedal a more normal feel. The second pair of pads were also operated by the handbrake. A further innovation was the fitting of disc brakes. Rolls-Royce were the last major British manufacturer to make the switch. This was because the company's engineers abhorred brake squeal, to which discs were particularly prone, and the

Opposite top: Two interior views of the Phantom V built for the Queen in 1960
Opposite: Profile of a 1960 Phantom V seven-seater limousine by Park Ward

Above: The Silver Shadow I received enthusiastic reviews when it appeared in 1965. This saloon was built in 1970

Rolls-Royce drum brakes were so good anyway. Working hand-in-hand with Ferodo, however, the company evolved a system that made the discs squeal-free. The discs were silenced by wrapping steel wire loosely around a groove cut into the periphery of each disc and retaining it with a clamp ring. It proved most effective.

The geometry of the new suspension was straightforward, consisting as it did of long trailing links at the rear and an unequal-length wishbone set-up at the front. Coil springs concentric with the shock-absorbers and hydraulic self-loading struts provided the suspension. The suspension subframes were most carefully tuned to the chassis. Delaney Gallay had produced special Vibrashock mountings (that looked like stainless-steel pan-scrubs) for the front anchorages of the rear suspension subframe. They were used in conjunction with little double-action shock-absorbers.

Under the bonnet the Silver Shadow was very much the same as the Silver Cloud III. It had the same compression ratio but there were a number of improvements. There were, for example, new cylinder heads with improved combustion chamber shapes, and the plugs were located above the exhaust manifold where they could be reached by opening the bonnet instead of having to remove the front wheels. High-pressure hydraulic pumps were driven off the camshaft.

By now we have come to accept the styling of the Shadow body, but when it first appeared the diehards decried its shape and there were slighting references to its resembling a tarted-up Peugeot 403. The designers had succeeded in making a car 4½in lower, 3¾in narrower and 6¾in shorter than the Silver Cloud III yet with more room than the model it superseded. It was wider inside and had 2in more interior space from front to rear. Structurally it was a steel monocoque. As is well known, this makes for a very much stiffer structure than a separate

chassis and body, and also saves weight. In view of the large number of extra mechanical components this was essential because the Shadow was so full of good works that it actually came out almost 100lb heavier than the larger Cloud III. This fact was reflected in the first road tests, which gave it a maximum of 115mph whereas the bulky Cloud III did 116mph. The older model took 19.2 seconds to accelerate from standstill to 80mph but the new car took 19.7 seconds. When the Silver Shadow was

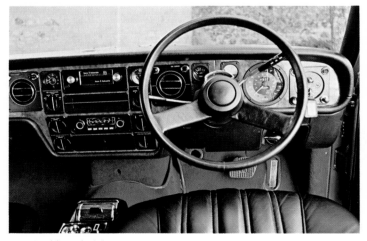

Top: Dashboard of the Camargue
Right: The Corniche was launched
in 1971 in two styles, saloon
and convertible

announced its price was £6,669 19s including purchase tax. Two years after its introduction the model was found, when tested, to give 12.2 miles per gallon.

Although there was widely expressed admiration for the design and execution of the Silver Shadow it was not without its critics. Murmurings persisted for a considerable time, in fact until the recirculating ball steering was replaced by a rack-and-pinion layout in 1977. The main burden of the criticism was lack of feel when going straight ahead. Admittedly this was disturbing on first acquaintance but drivers eventually got used to it. The company said that the car had been designed primarily for the American market and that that was how Cadillac customers liked it, but in Europe this was not accepted as a valid argument. Other criticisms were of road noise and body roll when cornering; and, if driven hard, the tyres wore out at an alarming rate. All these shortcomings were ironed out later.

Five years after the introduction of the Shadow came financial disaster and Rolls-Royce Limited, Europe's greatest aero-engine builder, suddenly found itself in the hands of a receiver. Allegations were made of extravagance, poor management and preoccupation with the wrong product, issues which are best discussed elsewhere, but after swift government intervention the aero-engine side of the company was enabled to remain in business as a state-run enterprise. Out of the ashes the car division arose in the new guise of Rolls-Royce Motors Limited, a separate, independent public company that would be responsible for its own profits, its own losses and with its own compact manufacturing unit at Crewe. What the new company had, as well, was a new managing director in David Plastow, the son of a motor engineer, who had been sales director in the former company.

Under Plastow's direction the cars were not only to become more European but also more saleable worldwide. One of the first announcements after the reorganization was the new Corniche model, which went on sale in 1971. At the same time it was announced that henceforth there would be a special, personal model such as the Corniche which would be the engineering and styling leader for production cars of the future. Thus the new Corniche had a large-capacity engine with the stroke lengthened to 3.9in to give a capacity of 6,750cc. Horsepower was not specified but it proved capable of propelling the car at more than 120mph and taking it from standstill to 80mph in 16.9 seconds. The body was a two-door creation by Mulliner Park Ward and was available as a hard top or a soft top. It was a beautifully finished personal motor car in the idiom of Claude Johnson's Continental.

All of the modifications incorporated and proved in the Corniche appeared in the Silver Shadow II in 1977. Just how much development had been done in 11 years of production, during which 24,000 Silver Shadows were produced, is shown by the fact that there were 2,000 engineering changes in all. The main modifications were alterations to the front suspension to allow the outside front wheel to develop more negative camber as the car rolled, and therefore improve stability; wide-rimmed wheels with low-profile tyres; and a revised front end with a slightly deeper radiator shell. A most important addition was an air dam under new-style front bumpers to improve stability at high speed.

Passenger comfort had been much enhanced by modifications to the air conditioning which was developed from the fully automatic system installed in the Corniche. This had temperature sensors located behind the rear bumper and inside the car and maintained the set temperature automatically. Moreover, all air coming into the car had to pass through the refrigeration unit and was therefore dehumidified. These latest changes give the car today a completely new identity when compared with the

1965 model. In a 1,400-mile test in 1974 the Corniche gave just on 12 miles to the gallon.

Perpetuating the policy of having a special-bodied car incorporating future developments, Rolls-Royce commissioned Pininfarina of Turin to design a new body on the Corniche chassis to be built by the Mulliner Park Ward division in London. Once again the new car, named Camargue, was a two-door personal motor car. Predictably, its styling attracted much criticism when it was first unveiled but it soon gained acceptance and the advantages of its greater internal accommodation and even further improved, solid state control air conditioning are appreciated by fortunate owners of this motor car.

In recent years the price of Rolls-Royce cars has risen steadily – but so has demand. In 1978 production exceeded 3,300 units and some 60 per cent were exported. In less than 10 years since the car division achieved a separate identity, Rolls-Royce Motors has become, for its size, the most profitable motor manufacturing company in Britain. It is an achievement that Charles Rolls and Henry Royce would have applauded.

Top: The Silver Shadow II has rack and pinion steering. The car shown here was built in 1978
Above: The Phantom VI is the most expensive Rolls-Royce

Top: A 1979 Silver Shadow II
Above: The Silver Wraith II was
introduced in 1977, the same year
that the Silver Shadow II made
its debut

The most famous and venerated
Rolls-Royce of all – AX201,
The Silver Ghost, built in 1907
to publicize the marque and
doing so magnificently still

TECHNICAL SPECIFICATIONS

In the 75 years since the first Rolls-Royce car was built in 1904, a total of 28 models have appeared from works at Manchester, Derby, Crewe and London in Britain and Springfield, Mass, in the United States. In the following section, illustrations of each model are accompanied by concise technical information.

10hp

This first Rolls-Royce model, 10 of which were built, was produced from 1904 to 1906.

Engine

Configuration Water-cooled, in-line two cylinders; two-throw three-bearing crankcase; splash lubrication with pump return to dash tank with sight feeds
Dimensions 3.75in × 5in (110.4cu in) or 3.94in × 5in (121.9cu in); 95.3mm × 127mm (1,809cc) or 100mm × 127mm (1,995cc)
Ignition Trembler coil and battery with standby battery
Carburation Royce single jet, based on Krebs
Power output Estimated 12bhp at 1,000rpm

Transmission

Gearbox Sliding pinion; three speeds and reverse; cardan shaft drive
Drive Cone clutch; open propeller shaft; pot joint and flex coupling
Axle Live, fully floating; straight cut bevels; spurwheel differential; high, low or medium ratio axles available
Speeds in gears Medium ratio: 1st 13mph; 2nd 22mph; 3rd 36mph

Chassis

Type Parallel girder with forged dumb-irons; engine subframe
Suspension Semi-elliptic all round
Brakes Footbrake for transmission (gearbox end); handbrake operating internal expanding drum brakes on rear wheels
Wheelbase 75in
Track 48in
Tyre size 810 × 90
Best-known body-styles Two-seater by Barker; four-seat tourer by Cann or Barker
Performance 39mph maximum with high axle ratio

Engine of a 1905 two-cylinder 10hp

The Science Museum in London owns this 1905 10hp

15hp

This was one of the first four models – 10hp, 15hp, 20hp and 30hp – that were commissioned by C. S. Rolls and Company from Royce Limited. The 15hp was made in 1905 and production numbered six. The first car of this model was presented to Dr Warre, headmaster of Eton, by old boys on his retirement in 1905.

Engine

Configuration Water-cooled; three cylinders in line; four main bearings; splash lubrication with return feed to tank
Dimensions 4in × 5in (188.5cu in); 101.6mm × 127mm (3,089cc)
Ignition High tension with single coil and trembler; standby battery
Carburation Royce-Krebs with automatic air bypass
Power output 15bhp at 1,000rpm nominal

Transmission

Gearbox Three speeds and reverse
Drive Cone clutch; cardan shaft; open propeller shaft
Axle Fully floating; spurwheel differential; three alternative ratios
Speeds in gears Medium ratio: 1st 13mph; 2nd 22mph; 3rd 32mph

Chassis

Type Parallel pressed side-members
Suspension Semi-elliptic on front; platform type at rear
Brakes Handbrake for rear; footbrake for transmission
Wheelbase 103in
Track 50in
Weight without body 1,568lb
Tyre size 810 × 90
Best-known body-styles Tourer, or double brougham
Performance 39½mph maximum with high ratio axle

The last 15hp three-cylinder Rolls-Royce to be built

20hp

The most successful of the four models first commissioned from Royce, the 20hp was produced in 1905 and 1906. All told, 40 were built. A car of this type won the 1906 Tourist Trophy with Rolls driving; the year before Percy Northey had been placed second. Three basic models were made: the light chassis, the TT Replica and the heavy chassis.

Engine

Configuration Water-cooled, in-line four cylinders; five main bearings; mechanically operated overhead inlet valves; side exhaust; splash lubrication with pump return to tank; drip feeds
Dimensions 4in × 5in (251.3cu in); 101.6mm × 127mm (4,118cc)
Ignition High tension with single coil and trembler; two batteries
Carburation Royce-Krebs carburettor with automatic air bypass
Power output Nominal 20bhp at 1,000rpm

Transmission

Gearbox Three speeds and reverse, except on Tourist Trophy model which had four speeds and reverse; direct drive on third, overdrive top
Drive Cone clutch; cardan shaft; open propeller shaft

Axle Fully floating; spurwheel differential; ratios: light 2.40, 2.60, 3; heavy 3, 3.25, 3.60
Speeds in gears Light: 52mph maximum; heavy: 47mph maximum

Chassis

Type Pressed steel; parallel side-members
Suspension Semi-elliptic on front; three-spring platform on rear
Brakes Handbrake for rear, footbrake for transmission
Wheelbase 106in or 114in
Track 52in (light); 56in (heavy)
Weight without body 1,624lb (light), 1,848lb (heavy)
Tyre sizes Light: 810 × 90 front, 810 × 100 rear; heavy: 870 × 90 front, 880 × 120 rear
Best-known body-styles Tourer, TT Replica, Roi-des-Belges

20hp four-cylinder of 1905–06

30hp

This, the largest of the first four Rolls-Royce models, was first shown at the Paris Salon in 1904 but was slow to reach production. When it was exhibited at the New York motor show in 1905 many orders were taken for it. Because of the lack of appreciation of six-cylinder camshaft problems at that time the engine was less smooth than it might have been. This model was superseded by the 40/50hp Silver Ghost. Production of the 30hp in 1905–06 totalled 37.

Engine

Configuration Six cylinders in line; water-cooled; overhead inlet and side exhaust valves; crankshaft with three sets of twin throws; splash lubrication with engine-driven pump return
Dimensions 4in × 5in (377cu in); 101.6mm × 127mm (6,177cc)
Ignition High-tension coil and trembler; commutator on dash
Carburation Royce-Krebs carburettor; automatic air bypass
Power output Nominal 30bhp at 1,000rpm

Transmission

Gearbox Four speeds and reverse; direct drive on third; overdrive top; ball bearing on main shafts
Drive Cone clutch; cardan shaft; open propeller shaft
Axle Fully floating ball bearings; spurwheel differential

Chassis

Type Pressed steel side-members
Suspension Semi-elliptic on front; three-spring platform type on rear
Brakes On rear only; transmission footbrake
Wheelbase 116½in (short), 118in (long)
Track 56in
Weight without body Short wheelbase: 2,072lb; long wheelbase: 2,128lb
Tyre sizes Short wheelbase: 870 × 90 front, 880 × 120 rear; long wheelbase: 880 × 120 front, 895 × 135 rear
Best-known body-styles Tourers and enclosed Pullman by Barker
Performance 55mph approximately with lightweight body

1905 30hp six-cylinder

Legalimit and Invisible Engine

These were designed to meet a passing fashion for a town car that would be an alternative to the electric brougham. Lord Northcliffe was the most notable of those who expressed the view that motorists would be happy with a vehicle which was incapable of exceeding the legal speed limit for cars of 20mph. Royce and Claude Johnson also tried to meet a demand for a car in which the engine was hidden. Commercially, these cars were the least successful of all Rolls-Royces, although the engine met the requirements very well indeed.

Engine

Configuration Side-valve eight-cylinder set in a vee at 90 degrees in two blocks of four; integral cast-iron blocks and heads on aluminium crankcase; hollow three-main bearing crankshaft (two plane); pressure lubrication
Dimensions $3\frac{1}{4}$in × $3\frac{1}{4}$in (215.7cu in); 82.6mm × 82.6mm (3,535cc)
Ignition One plug per cylinder; separate coil and trembler systems for each cylinder bank fired by two-tier distributor
Carburation Royce-Krebs single jet; semi-constant displacement

Transmission

Gearbox Three speeds and reverse; sliding mesh; direct drive top; in separate casing
Drive Cone clutch; open propeller shaft
Axle Fully floating; spurwheel differential

Speeds in gears On Legalimit with different governor settings: high setting, top 21mph; 2nd $13\frac{1}{2}$mph; bottom 8mph; low setting: top 26mph; 2nd 16mph; bottom $9\frac{1}{2}$mph

Chassis

Type Lightweight parallel girder
Suspension Semi-elliptic on front; platform type comprising two semi-elliptic and transverse springs on rear; axle located by torque stay
Brakes Handbrake-operated internal expanding on rear; footbrake to drum transmission brake
Wheelbase Legalimit: 106in; Invisible Engine 90in
Track 52in
Weight of typical car About 2,240lb
Tyre sizes Legalimit: 810 × 90 front, 810 × 100 rear; Invisible engine: 820 × 120 all round

Above: The Invisible Engine model
Opposite: The Legalimit

Silver Ghost (Britain)

The side-valve 40/50hp Ghost was undoubtedly Henry Royce's greatest design. It was the first model to be built at Derby and for the first few years was the only model due to lack of capital to finance tooling. Johnson persisted with the one-model policy until 1922. Chassis number 60551, registration AX201, was fitted with a Barker body painted silver, given silver-plated fittings and named The Silver Ghost. It was one of a number of 40/50s with similar names but this particular car became the most famous of all because of its 15,000 mile reliability run of 1907 and through its later career as a world-travelled ambassador for the Rolls-Royce company. Total production of the 40/50 Ghost numbered 6,173 between 1907 and 1925.

Engine

Configuration Six cylinders in line; L-head with two one-piece blocks and heads; side valves with exposed springs; seven bearing crankshaft; pressure lubrication; cast-iron pistons until 1919, aluminium standard thereafter
Dimensions 4½in × 4½in (429.4cu in); 114.3mm × 114.3mm (7,036cc); 1909: 4½in × 4¾in (453.3cu in); 114.3mm × 120.7mm (7,428cc)
Ignition Dual with magneto and trembler coil until 1919; magneto and fixed coil later
Carburation Rolls-Royce two-jet water-heated, semi-displacement, plus starting carburettor after 1921
Power Estimated 48bhp at 1,250rpm

Transmission

Gearbox Sliding pinion; 1st series: four speeds, overdrive top; 2nd series: three speeds; 3rd series: four speeds, direct top
Drive Cone clutch; cardan shaft; open propeller shaft and torque arm 1907–11; afterwards propeller shaft enclosed in torque tube
Axle Live, fully floating; spiral bevel; ratios: 1907, 2.89 or 2.12; 1910, 2.89 or 2.71; 1912, 2.89 or 3.06; 1919, 3.25; 1921–23, 3.47; an alternative of 3.71 was introduced in 1923

Chassis

Type Parallel girder; tubular cross-members; bell crank front engine mounting
Suspension Rear: 1907, platform type; 1908–11, three-quarter elliptic; 1912–25, cantilever; front: semi-elliptic; friction dampers
Brakes Internal expanding rear and transmission brake; after First World War concentric drums for handbrake and footbrake; 1924, four-wheel brakes with gearbox-driven servo
Wheelbase 1907: 135½in or 143½in; 1914: 143½in; 1923: 144in or 150½in
Track 56in
Weight of chassis 1907: 2,352lb or 2,520lb; thereafter 2,856lb
Weight of typical car 3,360lb
Tyre sizes 1907: 880 × 120 or 895 × 135 front, 875 × 105 or 880 × 120 rear; 1914: 895 × 135; 1923: 33 × 5
Better-known body-styles Barker tourer; Hooper landaulet; London-Edinburgh type scuttle tourer; Barker enclosed cabriolet

1920 Silver Ghost cabriolet de ville by Joseph Cockshoot

Silver Ghost (United States)

The object of making the 40/50 in America at Springfield, Mass, was to cut manufacturing costs and avoid hefty import duties. It was intended that the Springfield 40/50 should be identical to the Derby-built car but local conditions and customer preference soon enforced changes. Only the first few American-built cars were identical, thereafter they became progressively Americanized with Bosch magnetos, Delco coil ignition and Bijur generators, for example. Left-hand drive and a three-speed centre shift gearbox came in 1925. Production of this model, from 1921 to 1926, numbered 1,703.

Engine

Configuration Six cylinders in line; side valve, with one-piece blocks and heads cast in units of three; seven-bearing hollow crankshaft; aluminium pistons; valve stems and springs exposed until 1925; compression ratio 3.91:1
Dimensions $4\frac{1}{2}$in × $4\frac{3}{4}$in (453.3cu in); 114.3mm × 120.7mm (7,428cc)
Ignition Dual coil and magneto; double coil introduced in 1925
Carburation Rolls-Royce exhaust-heated two-jet semi-displacement, plus starting carburettor
Power output 86bhp at 2,250rpm

Transmission

Gearbox Separate sliding pinion; four speeds; direct drive top; three-speed centre change on left-hand-drive cars introduced in 1925
Drive Cone clutch; cardan shaft; gearbox to axle; enclosed shaft in tapered torque tube

Axle Fully floating; spiral bevel; spurwheel differential; ratio 3.25 on initial production; after 1922, 3.47, 3.71 or 3.25
Speeds in gears With 3.47 axle and four speeds: 1st 19mph; 2nd 29mph; 3rd 43mph; top 64mph; three speeds: 1st 22.3mph; 2nd 42.3mph; 3rd 64mph

Chassis

Type Parallel girder type; tubular cross-members; bell crank engine mountings
Suspension Semi-elliptic on front; cantilever on rear; friction dampers
Brakes On rear only; concentric drums for footbrake and handbrake; no servo
Wheelbase 144in or $150\frac{1}{2}$in
Track 56in
Weight of chassis 2,856lb
Weight of typical car 3,920lb
Tyre sizes 33 × 5 or 33 × 6.75
Better-known body-styles Piccadilly roadster; Brewster Pall Mall; Salamanca town car
Performance Maximum about 65mph with touring body

Opposite top: 1924 Silver Ghost Salamanca with Rolls-Royce Custom Coach Work by New Haven
Opposite: 1923 Silver Ghost, also with Custom Coach ork by New Haven

Twenty

This model was introduced to meet requests for a smaller, less expensive car in keeping with the trend after the First World War towards smaller cars for a wider market. Construction was simplified in order to reduce costs – single ignition was fitted, for example, and the three-speed gearbox had central change – but standards of workmanship were not compromised. Price of the chassis on introduction was £1,100. During its production life, 1922–29, 2,940 were built.

Engine

Configuration Overhead valve six cylinders in line; monobloc, cast-iron cylinder casting spigoted into cast aluminium crankcase; separate cast-iron head; push-rod operated valves; seven-bearing hollow crankshaft; pressure lubrication; gear-driven camshaft
Dimensions 3in × 4½in (190.9cu in); 76.2mm × 114.3mm (3,127cc)
Ignition Single coil with option of standby magneto, which became standard after 1923
Carburation Rolls-Royce two-jet; constant displacement

Transmission

Gearbox Three speeds and reverse; centre change 1922–25; four speeds with right-hand change 1925–29; both had direct drive on top; in unit with engine
Drive Single dry-plate clutch; open driveshaft
Axle Fully floating; spiral bevel; ratio 4.6:1 or 4.4:1
Speeds in gears 1st 13mph; 2nd 28mph; 3rd 40mph; top 62mph

Chassis

Type Parallel girder; open section with tubular cross-members
Suspension All round semi-elliptic springs with friction shock-absorbers 1922–26; thereafter hydraulic dampers on the front axle only
Brakes Rear drum brakes with handbrake operating duplicate shoes in same drums 1922–25; after that four-wheel drum brakes with Rolls-Royce servo
Wheelbase 129in
Track 54in
Weight of chassis 2,305lb as originally designed; later gained 300lb
Weight of typical car 3,215lb (Barker tourer)
Tyre size Originally 32 × 4.5; 1927: 21 × 5.25; later 600 × 20
Some better-known body-styles Barker standard tourer and saloon
Performance Maximum of early models was about 62mph; later models were capable of 70mph with light bodywork but the emphasis was always on silence and smoothness of the ride

Opposite top left: Coupe by Caffyns on a Twenty of 1927
Opposite top right: 1923 Twenty cabriolet by Windovers
Opposite: Weymann-style saloon by Caffyns on a 1929 Twenty

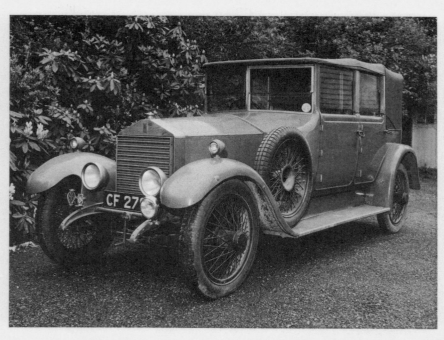

Phantom I (Britain)

Introduced in 1925 to meet the need for a modern, ohv, large car in the Rolls-Royce range, the Phantom I (known at the time as the New Phantom) remained in production until 1929. A total of 2,212 were built. It was virtually the Silver Ghost model with a more modern, long stroke, ohv engine. It was one of the more short-lived models. One reason for its replacement in 1929 by the Phantom II was that the engine proved too fast for the elderly Ghost chassis which, with front brakes, suffered from chronic axle tramp that Derby toiled in vain to subdue.

Engine

Configuration Six cylinders in line; two blocks of three with one-piece detachable iron (later aluminium) head; push-rod overhead valves; roller tappets; seven-bearing hollow crankshaft; mounted directly in the frame at three points
Dimensions $4\frac{1}{4}$in × $5\frac{1}{2}$in (468.1cu in); 108mm × 139.7mm (7,668cc)
Ignition Dual with magneto and coil; 12 plugs on one side of head
Carburation Rolls-Royce two-jet; exhaust-heated; semi-constant displacement; starting carburettor
Power output 108bhp at 2,300rpm

Transmission

Gearbox Separate, four-speed, sliding mesh; direct drive top incorporating brake servo
Drive Single plate clutch and cardan shaft; propeller shaft enclosed in torque tube
Axle Fully floating; spiral bevel; spurwheel differential; ratio 3.47 : 1, later 3.25 : 1
Speeds in gears At 2,250rpm: 1st 19mph; 2nd 29mph; 3rd 43mph; top 64mph

Chassis

Type Parallel girder; tubular cross-members
Suspension Semi-elliptic at front; cantilever at rear; early production had friction dampers; later cars had hydraulic on front, then hydraulic on rear
Brakes Four-wheel drum; mechanical servo handbrake on concentric rear drums
Wheelbase $143\frac{1}{4}$in or $150\frac{1}{2}$in
Track 56in (short chassis), $57\frac{1}{2}$in (long chassis)
Weight of chassis 4,000lb
Weight of typical car 5,800lb
Tyre sizes 33 × 5; 700 × 21 (1928)
Better-known body-styles Barker barrel-body tourer; Barker Pullman limousine; Gurney Nutting Weymann saloon
Performance By taking the engine up to 3,000rpm a maximum speed of 85mph should have been possible with the lighter type of body

Opposite top: An experimental Phantom I
Opposite: 1925 Phantom I sedanca de ville by Caffyns

Phantom I (United States)

Because of the need to redesign the engine with the carburettor and manifolding on the left-hand side the first Springfield Phantom I was not completed until 1926. This major change, which also required the engine-speed governor to be moved over, was to allow the use of the expensive-to-make hand control linkage based on the steering column. This car differed from its British counterpart in that early production vehicles had two-wheel brakes and there were, in addition, many components from US manufacturers. Production ceased in 1931 when more than 1,240 had been built.

Engine

Configuration Six cylinders in line; two blocks of three with one-piece detachable head; cast-iron blocks; aluminium crankcase; cast-iron head, later aluminium; push-rod overhead valves; roller tappets; seven-bearing hollow crankshaft; three-point mounting
Dimensions $4\frac{1}{4}$in × $5\frac{1}{2}$in (468.1cu in); 108mm × 139.7mm (7,672cc)
Ignition Dual Delco coil
Carburation Rolls-Royce two jet, semi-constant displacement; starting carburettor
Power output 108bhp at 2,300rpm

Transmission

Gearbox Separate three-speed sliding mesh; direct drive top; centre change
Drive Single-plate clutch and cardan shaft; propeller shaft inside tapered torque tube
Axle Fully floating; spiral bevel; spurwheel differential; ratios 3.71, 3.47, 3.25
Speeds in gears With 3.47 axle at 2,250rpm: 1st 22.7mph; 2nd 43mph; 3rd 63.9mph

Chassis

Type Parallel girder; tubular cross-members
Suspension Semi-elliptic on front; cantilever at rear; first 240 chassis had friction dampers; later cars had front hydraulic dampers
Brakes Early chassis had rear drums (concentric) only; afterwards, four-wheel drum brakes with Rolls-Royce mechanical servo built into American three-speed gearbox
Wheelbase $143\frac{1}{2}$in or $146\frac{1}{2}$in
Track 57in or $58\frac{1}{2}$in
Weight of chassis Approximately 4,000lb
Weight of typical car 5,700lb (Pickwick sedan)
Tyre size 33 × 6.75; 7 × 20 later
Some better-known body-styles Pall Mall by Brewster and Rolls-Royce Custom Coach Work; Newmarket and Salamanca by Brewster
Performance A light-bodied car would have probably been capable of 80mph but a typical maximum would have been 70mph

Opposite top: 1929 Phantom I York roadster by Brewster
Opposite: 1929 Phantom I Huntington saloon by Brewster

20/25

This development of the Twenty was the best-selling Rolls-Royce between the First and Second World Wars. As a companion model to the Phantom II it was given a taller radiator with vertical radiator shutters, large section tyres, improved brakes and better chassis lubrication. Improved crankshaft balancing allowed the engine to run faster. The production period, 1929–36, coincided with big improvements in the six-cylinder 20hp engine, and later models of the 20/25 were considerably faster than earlier ones.

Engine

Configuration Overhead valve six cylinders in line; monobloc, cast-iron cylinder casting spigoted into cast aluminium crankcase; separate cast-iron head; push-rod operated valves; seven-bearing, hollow crankshaft; pressure lubrication; gear-driven camshaft and ancillaries; incorporated the 'eight weight' crankshaft balance scheme; cam balancer introduced in 1934
Dimensions $3\frac{1}{4}$in × $4\frac{1}{2}$in (224cu in); 82.6mm × 114.3mm (3,675cc)
Ignition Single coil ignition with standby magneto
Carburation Rolls-Royce two-jet; after 1934 SU type

Transmission

Gearbox Four speeds and reverse; in unit with engine; synchromesh on 3rd and top in 1932
Drive Single dry-plate clutch; open drive shaft; Hardy Spicer shaft after 1934
Axle Fully floating; spiral bevel; hypoid axle introduced in 1936; ratio 4.55
Speeds in gears 1st 18mph; 2nd 32mph; 3rd 53mph; top 73.32mph (1935)

Chassis

Type Parallel girder; tubular cross-members; engine and gearbox in subframe; three-point, diamond and flexible subframe mountings
Suspension All round semi-elliptic springs; hydraulic shock-absorbers; manual control after 1934
Brakes Four-wheel internal expanding with separate shoes in rear drums for handbrake; Rolls-Royce gearbox-driven servo
Wheelbase 129in
Track 56in
Weight of chassis 2,653lb rising to 2,900lb
Weight of typical car 4,218lb (1935 Park Ward saloon)
Tyre size 600 × 19
Some better-known body-styles Park Ward four-door sports saloon; Barker limousine and owner-drive saloon
Performance Maximum 73.32mph; 0–50mph in 21 seconds; 0–60mph in 31.4 seconds (1935)

Opposite top: 1934 20/25hp with coachwork by Arthur Mulliner
Opposite: 1933 20/25hp sports coupe by Barker

Phantom II

The first all-new 40/50 since the 40/50 Ghost, the Phantom II was introduced to combat sales competition from the Bentley $6\frac{1}{2}$-litre and 8-litre models and other makes that were of more modern conception than the old 40/50. The new chassis was of the same general configuration as that of the Twenty and almost all sign of the front axle tramp, the big bugbear of the Phantom I, was eliminated. This car was the basis of the Continental model and is regarded by many as the finest Rolls-Royce model of all. It was produced between 1929 and 1935; 1,767 were built.

Engine

Configuration Six cylinders in line; two blocks of three; cast-iron cylinders on aluminium crankcase and one-piece aluminium head; push-rod operated, in-line overhead valves; four-point mounting
Dimensions $4\frac{1}{4}$in × $5\frac{1}{2}$in (468.1cu in); 108mm × 139.7mm (7,668cc)
Ignition Dual with magneto and coil firing together; automatic advance and retard with overriding hand control
Carburation Rolls-Royce two-jet; semi-displacement; starting carburettor; water-heated up-pipe on early production; after 1930 exhaust heated

Transmission

Gearbox Four speeds; in unit with engine; constant mesh until 1933 when synchro introduced on top and 3rd; synchro on 2nd was introduced in 1935
Drive Single dry-plate clutch and open propeller shaft
Axle Fully floating; hypoid bevel; ratios 3.73 (1929–34), 3.42 (1934–35); 3.42 optional from 1930 to 1934
Speeds in gears With 3.42 axle: 1st 29mph; 2nd 50mph; 3rd 75mph; top 92mph

Chassis

Type Parallel girder with tubular and girder cross-members; upswept over rear axle; centralized lubrication
Suspension Semi-elliptic front and rear; shock-absorbers' arms acted as radius rods controlling front axle twist through triangular link; double piston hydraulic dampers with, from 1933, variable loading automatically increased with road speed
Brakes On all four wheels; internal expanding; Rolls-Royce servo; handbrake operating separate shoes
Wheelbase 144in (short chassis and Continental model) or 150in
Track $58\frac{1}{2}$in
Weight of chassis 3,810lb
Weight of typical car 5,488lb (Continental with owner-driver body)
Tyre size 21in early on; 20in (1930) and 19in (1933)
Some better-known body-styles Barker close-coupled touring saloon; Park Ward Continental coupe; Barker torpedo tourer
Performance For Park Ward Continental: maximum 92.3mph; 0–50mph in 14.6 seconds; 0–60mph in 19.4 seconds

1930 Phantom II sedanca de ville by Hooper

Phantom III

Designed to meet the growing competition from European and American manufacturers with V12, V8 and in-line eight-cylinder power units which were making the Phantom II look out of date in both design and refinement, the Phantom III was built between 1935 and 1939 and total production numbered 710. The decision to go to a V12 was Royce's last major contribution and the actual design work was completed by his team of designers after his death.

Engine

Configuration V12 set at 60 degrees; light-alloy block and head with cast-iron wet liners; overhead valves with single camshaft; hydraulic tappets at first; solid tappets from 1938; seven-bearing crankshaft
Dimensions 3.25in × 4.5in (169.64cu in); 82.5mm × 114.3mm (7,338cc)
Ignition Dual coil and distributors; two plugs per cylinder
Carburation Dual downdraught of the Stromberg type

Transmission

Gearbox Separate; four speeds; synchromesh on 2nd, 3rd and top
Drive Single dry-plate clutch; cardan shaft; open propeller shaft
Axle Fully floating live axle; hypoid bevel differential; ratio 4.25 :1
Speeds in gears 2nd 44mph; 3rd 73mph

Chassis

Type Pressed-steel ladder type with cruciform
Suspension Front: unequal length wishbone; oil immersed coil spring; rear: semi-elliptic
Brakes On all four wheels; mechanically operated from gearbox servo
Wheelbase 142in
Track 60½in (front), 62½in (rear)
Weight of chassis 4,050lb without spare tyre and tools
Tyre size 700 × 18 or 750 × 18
Better-known body-styles Park Ward limousine and sedanca de ville; Hooper sedanca de ville
Performance For Park Ward limousine: best speed 91.84mph; maximum in 3rd 73mph; 0–50mph in 12.6 seconds; 0–60mph in 16.8 seconds

The Phantom III, introduced in 1935

25/30

This car, introduced in 1936, marked a further step in the development of the Twenty with an engine stretched to 4,257cc in the 20/25 chassis. The same engine with different carburation and a higher compression ratio was used in the $4\frac{1}{4}$-litre Bentley. The wane of Royce's influence was seen in the use of proprietary carburettor, propeller shaft, SU pumps, Bijur starter and Lucas electrical equipment. The extra power from the 25/30 engine was almost totally offset by heavier chassis and coachwork.

Engine

Configuration Overhead valve six cylinders in line with cast-iron block spigoted into the aluminium crankcase; fully balanced, hollow, seven-bearing crankshaft on aluminium-tin bearings; camshaft balancer and low inertia crankshaft damper; carburettor mounted on right-hand side of engine
Dimensions $3\frac{1}{2}$in × $4\frac{1}{2}$in (259.8cu in); 88.9mm × 114.3mm (4,257cc)
Ignition Single coil with automatic advance and retard; standby magneto abandoned
Carburation Zenith-Stromberg downdraught
Power output Approximately 115bhp at 4,500rpm

Transmission

Gearbox Four-speed synchromesh on top and 3rd; in unit with engine
Drive Single dry-plate clutch and open, needle roller (Hardy Spicer) propeller shaft

Axle Fully floating; hypoid bevel; ratio 4.55:1
Speeds in gears Estimated 1st 22mph; 2nd 37mph; 3rd 60mph; top 80mph

Chassis

Type Parallel girder with tubular cross-members; pedal-operated central lubrication system
Suspension Semi-elliptic all round; hydraulic, remotely controlled shock-absorbers with speed responsive or hand control
Brakes Drum type on all four wheels with separate handbrake shoes for rear drums; Rolls-Royce servo assistance
Wheelbase 132in
Track $56\frac{1}{3}$in
Weight of chassis 2,930lb
Weight of typical car 4,300lb
Tyre size 600 × 19
Some better-known body-styles Park Ward owner-driver saloon, enclosed and touring limousines

Opposite top: 1936 25/30hp saloon by Mann Egerton
Opposite: 1936 25/30 touring limousine by Windovers

Wraith

Announced in 1938 as a companion model to the Phantom III it included many features of that car such as independent front suspension and light-alloy engine. Although it was offered 'chassis only', a number of standard bodies were in fact available. It was a slower, more refined counterpart to the Bentley Mk V. Production in 1938 and 1939 totalled 491.

Engine

Configuration In-line six-cylinder; push-rod, overhead valve, cross-flow head; light alloy; separate cylinder block with cast-iron wet liners; light-alloy head with bronze valve inserts
Dimensions $3\frac{1}{2}$in × $4\frac{1}{2}$in (259.8cu in); 88.9mm × 114.3mm (4,257cc)
Ignition Single coil; automatic advance and retard; standby coil
Carburation Single downdraught Solex; accelerator pump; Rolls-Royce air cleaner and silencer

Transmission

Gearbox Four speeds and reverse; direct drive top; synchromesh on 2nd, 3rd and top
Drive Single dry-plate clutch and open propeller shaft to live axle
Axle Fully floating; hypoid bevel; ratio 4.25 : 1
Speeds in gears 70mph in 3rd

Chassis

Type Box section ladder type with central cruciform bracing
Suspension Front: unequal length semi-trailing wishbone; coil springs; rear: semi-elliptic springs; variable rate shock-absorbers
Wheelbase 136in
Track $58\frac{1}{2}$in (front), $59\frac{1}{2}$in (rear)
Weight without body 3,038lb with fuel and water but without spare
Weight of typical car Approximately 4,000lb
Tyre size 650 × 17
Better-known body-styles Park Ward four-light touring saloon; H. J. Mulliner four-light touring saloon; Park Ward limousine
Performance Maximum about 85mph; standing quarter-mile in 25 seconds; 0–30mph in 8 seconds; 0–50mph in 16.4 seconds

1938 Wraith sedanca de ville by Park Ward

Silver Wraith I

This was the first Rolls-Royce to appear after the Second World War and it featured a completely new design. The inlet-over-exhaust engine allowed the use of larger valves and 'leading link' independent front suspension. Offered as a chassis only it was regarded as a postwar replacement for the Phantom III. Production from 1947 until 1959 exceeded 1,700.

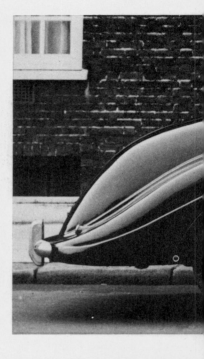

Engine

Configuration F-head in-line six-cylinder; one-piece block and crankcase; aluminium sump; seven-bearing, hollow, fully balanced crankshaft with low-inertia damper; Vandervell shell bearings of copper-lead-indium; cross-flow head; spring diaphragm flywheel
Dimensions $3\frac{1}{2}$in × $4\frac{1}{2}$in (259.8cu in); 88.9mm × 114.3mm (4,257cc); 1951: $3\frac{5}{8}$in × $4\frac{1}{2}$in (278.7cu in); 92.1mm × 114.3mm (4,566cc); 1955: $3\frac{3}{4}$in × $4\frac{1}{2}$in (298.2cu in); 95.25mm × 114.3mm (4,887cc)
Ignition Single coil with automatic advance and retard
Carburation Two-stroke downdraught Stromberg or single downdraught Zenith; twin SU pumps
Power output 122bhp at 4,400rpm

Transmission

Gearbox Rolls-Royce four-speed; synchromesh on 2nd, 3rd and top; option of RR–GM Hydramatic after 1952
Drive Single dry-plate clutch on manual transmission; open, two-piece propeller shaft with floating steady bearing
Axle Semi-floating hypoid; ratio 3.73 : 1

standard; 3.42 optional; 4.25 : 1 on E-series cars
Speeds in gears 1st 24mph; 2nd 44mph; 3rd 68mph; top 84mph (1949)

Chassis

Type Girder type tapering to front; open section side-members; cruciform bracing; three-point, rubber-mounted engine; centralized lubrication
Suspension Front: semi-leading link independent with coil springs; rear: semi-elliptic springs; fixed setting hydraulic shock-absorbers
Brakes Four-wheel, cast-iron drums; Rolls-Royce-driven servo; hydraulic operation to front brakes
Wheelbase 127in or 133in
Track 58in (front), 60in or 64in (rear)
Weight of chassis About 3,200lb for short wheelbase
Weight of typical car 4,732lb (short wheelbase sedanca de ville)
Tyre size 17 × 50; later 16 × 6.5
Some better-known body-styles H. J. Mulliner sedanca de ville; Hooper touring limousine
Performance 0–50mph in 17.2 seconds; 0–60mph in 24 seconds; 0–70mph in 37.4 seconds

Opposite top: 1953 Silver Wraith special clubman by Freestone and Webb
Opposite: 1948 Silver Wraith saloon by James Young

Silver Dawn

Introduced in 1949 to satisfy American demand for a Rolls-Royce equivalent of the Bentley Mk VI with standard steel body, the Silver Dawn was not offered on the domestic market in Britain until 1953 by which time the Bentley R-type had been announced with a 4,566cc engine and all right-hand versions of the Dawn were equivalent to this model. Compared with the Bentley the Silver Dawn had a lower compression ratio and a fixed-choke Stromberg carburettor to improve low-speed flexibility. By the time production ended in 1955 a total of 760 had been built.

Engine

Configuration F-head, in-line, six-cylinder; one-piece cast-iron block and crankcase; light-alloy head and sump; seven-bearing, hollow, fully balanced crankshaft with low-inertia damper; Vandervell copper-lead-indium shell bearings; spring diaphragm flywheel
Dimensions $3\frac{1}{2}$in × $4\frac{1}{2}$in (259.8cu in); 88.9mm × 114.3mm (4,257cc); 1951: $3\frac{5}{8}$in × $4\frac{1}{2}$in (278.7cu in); 92.1mm × 114.3mm (4,566cc)
Ignition Single coil with automatic advance and retard
Carburation Two-choke downdraught Stromberg fed by twin SU pumps
Power output 122bhp at 4,400rpm (4,257cc engine)

Transmission

Gearbox Four speeds and reverse; synchromesh on 2nd, 3rd and top; optional Rolls-Royce-built Hydramatic four-step transmission after 1952
Drive Single dry-plate clutch; open propeller shaft (manual box)

Axle Semi-floating; hypoid bevel; ratio 3.73 : 1 standard; from 1954 ratio 3.42 : 1 available
Speeds in gears 1st 16mph; 2nd 40mph; 3rd 59mph; top 86.5mph (4,566cc engine, 1953)

Chassis

Type Girder side-members with central cruciform bracing
Suspension Front: unequal-length wishbones and coil spring; semi-leading link geometry; hydraulic shock-absorbers; rear: semi-elliptic; remote control hydraulic shock-absorbers
Wheelbase 120in
Track $56\frac{1}{2}$in (front), $58\frac{5}{8}$in (rear)
Weight of chassis 3,575lb
Brakes Drum type on all wheels; Rolls-Royce mechanical servo with hydraulic operation to front brakes; separate handbrake system
Tyre size 500 × 16
Better-known body-styles Standard steel saloon; Park Ward drophead
Performance Standing quarter-mile in 20.4 seconds; 0–50mph in 11.4 seconds; 0–60mph in 16.2 seconds

*Opposite top: 1954 Silver Dawn saloon by James Young
Opposite: 1952 Silver Dawn special drop head coupe by H. J. Mulliner*

Phantom IV

Built exclusively for royalty and heads of state it is the largest car to be built by Rolls-Royce. It was based on a lengthened Silver Wraith chassis and was propelled by an eight-cylinder, in-line engine (known as the B-series) that was developed before the Second World War as a car engine and then adapted for military use. The first of this model was built for Princess Elizabeth in 1950, marking official acceptance of the Rolls-Royce as the royal car. Production of the Phantom IV ended in 1956.

Engine

Configuration F-head, eight-cylinders in line; one-piece cast-iron block and crankcase with light-alloy head and sump; nine-bearing, hollow, fully balanced crankcase running on Vandervell copper-lead-indium shell bearings
Dimensions $3\frac{1}{2}$in × $4\frac{1}{2}$in (346.4cu in); 88.9mm × 114.3mm (5,675cc)
Ignition Single coil and distributor; automatic advance and retard
Carburation Dual-choke, downdraught Stromberg

Transmission

Gearbox Four speeds and reverse; synchromesh on 2nd, 3rd and top; in unit with engine
Drive Single dry-plate clutch; open, divided propeller shaft
Axle Semi-floating; hypoid bevel; ratio 4.25 : 1

Chassis

Type Girder, open-section side-members; midships cruciform bracing; centralized lubrication system
Suspension Front: unequal-length wishbones and coil springs; semi-leading link geometry; hydraulic shock-absorbers; rear: semi-elliptic leaf springs; remotely controlled hydraulic shock-absorbers
Brakes Drum type on all wheels; Rolls-Royce mechanical servo; separate handbrake system operating on rear wheels
Wheelbase 145in
Track $58\frac{1}{2}$in (front), 63in (rear)
Tyre size 800 × 17

*Opposite top: 1952 Phantom I armour-plated cabriolet built for General Franco of Spain
Opposite: 1953 Phantom IV limousine by Hooper*

Silver Cloud I

First announced in 1955 the Silver Cloud series was a complete redesign with a new chassis, new standard body, larger engine and automatic transmission as standard (there was no option of a manual gearbox). It was progressively refined up to Silver Cloud III form with the option of power steering and air conditioning. Production of the Silver Cloud I ended in 1959.

Engine

Configuration F-head, in-line six-cylinder; one-piece cast-iron block and crankcase; light-alloy head and sump; improved head with half of induction manifold formed in head; seven-bearing, hollow, fully balanced crankshaft; Vandervell bearings; low-inertia damper; spring diaphragm flywheel
Dimensions $3\frac{3}{4}$in × $4\frac{1}{2}$in (298.2cu in); 95.25mm × 114.3mm (4,887cc)
Ignition Single coil; automatic advance and retard
Carburation Twin SUs; automatic starting device

Transmission

Gearbox Rolls-Royce-GM Hydramatic four-step; fluid coupling
Drive Two-piece propeller shaft with flexibly mounted support
Axle Semi-floating; hypoid bevel; ratio 3.42:1
Speeds in gears 1st 24mph; 2nd 34mph; 3rd 63mph; top 106mph (1958)

Chassis

Type Box girder type with cruciform bracing; tapered in plan; rear springs inside side-members and Z-bar location for axle
Suspension Front: unequal-length wishbones and coil springs; semi-trailing geometry; hydraulic shock-absorbers; rear: semi-elliptic with remote-control shock-absorbers
Brakes Drum type on all wheels; all hydraulically operated by Rolls-Royce mechanical servo; hydro-mechanical rear system
Wheelbase 123in or 127in
Track 58in
Weight of typical car 4,228lb
Better-known body-styles Standard steel saloon; James Young saloon and coupe
Performance Standing quarter-mile in 18.8 seconds; 0–50mph in 9.4 seconds; 0–60mph in 13 seconds; 0–100mph in 50.6 seconds

Opposite top: 1956 Silver Cloud I saloon by James Young
Opposite: 1956 Silver Cloud I special two light drop head coupe by H. J. Mulliner

Silver Cloud II

In principle the Silver Cloud II was a Cloud I with the V8 light-alloy engine introduced in September 1959. Power-assisted steering became standard equipment using a hydraulically assisted cam and roller system. An improved fresh air ventilating system was installed and the optional air-conditioning system was moved from the boot to inside the right-hand front wing. Production of this model ended in 1962.

Engine

Configuration Eight cylinders in vee; light-alloy block and crankcase with wet liners; light-alloy head with inserted valve seats; push-rod operated, in-line overhead valves with hydraulic, self-adjusting tappets; five main bearing, solid, two-plane crankshaft
Dimensions 4.1in × 3.6in (380cu in); 104.4mm × 91.44mm (6,230cc)
Ignition Single coil; automatic advance and retard
Carburation Two 1.75in SUs on cast manifold
Power output Estimated 185bhp at 4,500rpm

Transmission

Gearbox Rolls-Royce-GM Hydramatic four-step automatic; fluid coupling
Drive Gearbox in unit with engine; split propeller shaft with flexibly mounted support
Axle Semi-floating; hypoid bevel; ratio

3.08 : 1
Speeds in gears 1st 21mph; 2nd 50mph; 3rd 70mph; top 113.1mph

Chassis

Type Box girder with cruciform bracing; tapered in plan with rear springs inboard of side-members; Z-bar axle location; cam and roller power steering standard
Suspension Front: unequal-length wishbones and coil springs; semi-trailing geometry; hydraulic shock-absorbers; rear: semi-elliptic springs with remote-control shock-absorbers
Brakes Drums on all wheels; Rolls-Royce mechanical servo operation through hydraulic front and hydro-mechanical rear system
Wheelbase 123in or 127in
Weight of typical car 4,522lb
Tyre size 820 × 15
Performance Standing quarter-mile in 18.2 seconds; 0–50mph in 8.3 seconds; 0–60mph in 11.5 seconds; 0–100mph in 38.5 seconds

Opposite top: 1961 Silver Cloud II drop head coupe by H. J. Mulliner
Opposite: 1961 Silver Cloud II four-door cabriolet by H. J. Mulliner

Phantom V

This replacement for the Silver Wraith provided a long-wheelbase chassis for specialized coachwork incorporating features of the Silver Cloud in the shape of the box-section girder chassis and the Silver Cloud II, whose V8 engine was adopted. The Z-bar axle location of the Silver Cloud back axle was replaced by a single radius rod and by mounting the rear axle asymmetrically on the springs. Production of the Phantom V lasted from 1959 to 1968 and a total of 832 were built.

Engine

Configuration Eight cylinders in vee; light-alloy block and crankcase with wet liners; alloy head with in-line valves in pentroof combustion chambers; push-rod valve operation with hydraulic tappets
Dimensions 4.1in × 3.6in (380cu in); 104.4mm × 91.4mm (6,230cc)
Ignition Single coil; automatic advance and retard
Carburation Two SU HD8s fed by twin SU petrol pumps
Power output Estimated 200bhp at 4,500rpm

Transmission

Gearbox Rolls-Royce-GM Hydramatic, four-step with fluid coupling
Drive Gearbox in unit with engine; divided propeller shaft
Axle Semi-floating; hypoid bevel; live axle; ratio 3.89:1

Chassis

Type Box section girder type with cruciform bracing
Suspension Front: unequal-length, semi-trailing wishbones; hydraulic shock-absorbers; rear: semi-elliptic, inboard mounted springs; remote-control shock-absorbers; radius rod location
Brakes Drum type with Rolls-Royce mechanical servo
Wheelbase 144in
Track 60$\frac{7}{8}$in (front), 74in (rear)
Weight of chassis 5,600lb
Tyre size 890 × 15
Better-known body-styles Limousines by Park Ward, James Young and Hooper

Opposite top: 1960 Phantom V built for the Queen
Opposite: 1962 Phantom V limousine by Chapron

Silver Cloud III

Characteristics of this model included twin head-lamps, a lower bonnet line and higher wings without side-lamps. Power was increased by 8 per cent and extra inside space was attained by changes to the seats. The Silver Cloud III remained in production from 1962 until 1966.

Engine

Configuration Eight cylinders in vee; light-alloy block and crankcase with wet liners; light-alloy head with inserted valve seats; push-rod operated, in-line overhead valves with hydraulic, self-adjusting tappets; five main bearing, solid, two-plane crankshaft
Dimensions 4.1in × 3.6in (380cu in); 104.4mm × 91.44mm (6,230cc)
Ignition Single coil with automatic advance and retard
Carburation Two 1.75in SUs on cast manifold
Power output Estimated 200bhp at 4,500rpm

Transmission

Gearbox Rolls-Royce-GM Hydramatic four-step automatic with fluid coupling
Drive Gearbox in unit with engine; split propeller shaft with flexibly mounted support
Axle Semi-floating; hypoid bevel; ratio 3.08:1
Speeds in gears 1st 25mph; 2nd 40mph; 3rd 72mph; top 115.8mph

Chassis

Type Box girder type with cruciform bracing; tapered in plan with rear springs inboard of side-members; Z-bar axle location; power steering; cam and roller standard
Suspension Front: unequal-length wishbones and coil springs; semi-trailing geometry; hydraulic shock-absorbers; rear: semi-elliptic springs with remote-control shock-absorbers
Brakes Drums on all wheels; Rolls-Royce mechanical servo operation through hydraulic front and hydro-mechanical rear system
Wheelbase 123in or 127in
Weight of typical car 4,522lb
Tyre size 820 × 15
Performance Standing quarter-mile in 17.7 seconds; 0–50mph in 7.7 seconds; 0–60mph in 10.8 seconds; 0–100mph ir 34.2 seconds

Opposite top: 1965 Silver Cloud III standard saloon
Opposite: 1964 Silver Cloud III by Park Ward

Silver Shadow I

Technically the most advanced Rolls-Royce ever produced having independent suspension on all four wheels with ride-levelling and a full power braking system with disc brakes, the Silver Shadow I remained in production from 1965 until 1977. Although lower, narrower and shorter than the Silver Cloud this model had increased passenger space and an enlarged luggage boot. Although the most adventurous design ever to be approved by the company it has been the most commercially successful Rolls-Royce model to date.

Engine

Configuration Eight cylinders in vee; light-alloy block and crankcase with wet liners; alloy head with in-line valves and pentroof combustion chambers; push-rod valve operation with hydraulic tappets; solid, five main bearing, two-plane crankshaft
Dimensions 4.1in × 3.6in (380cu in): 104.4mm × 91.4mm (6,230cc); 1970: 4.1in × 3.9in (411.9cu in); 104.4mm × 99mm (6,750cc)
Ignition Single coil with automatic advance and retard
Carburation Two diaphragm type SU HD8s fed by twin SU electric pumps
Power output Estimated 200bhp at 4,500rpm (6,230cc engine); 220bhp at 4,500rpm (6,750cc engine)

Transmission

Gearbox Rolls-Royce-GM Hydramatic, four-step automatic with fluid coupling; 1965 (export only): GM three-speed with torque convertor; UK models had this transmission in 1968
Drive Gearbox in unit with engine; one-piece propeller shaft
Axle Rubber-mounted final drive (hypoid bevel); universally jointed drive shafts; ratio 3.08 : 1
Speeds in gears 1st 24mph; 2nd 43mph; 3rd 72mph; top 115mph (short chassis)

Chassis

Type In unit with body; engine, front suspension and rear suspension carried on separate subframes
Suspension Front: unequal-length wishbones and coil springs; 1in hydraulic height correction; rear: semi-trailing links and coil springs with 3in height adjustment from power hydraulic system; power assisted, re-circulating ball steering
Brakes Front and rear Rolls-Royce-Girling discs; power assistance from 2,000psi hydraulic system; separate hydrostatic rear system
Wheelbase 119½in or 124in
Track 57½in
Weight of complete car 4,546lb (short chassis)
Tyre size 845 × 15; 205 × 15 (1972)
Performance Standing quarter-mile in 17.6 seconds; 0–50mph in 7.8 seconds; 0–60mph in 10.9 seconds; 0–100mph in 37.8 seconds (short chassis)

Opposite top: 1970 Silver Shadow I
Opposite: 1976 Silver Shadow I with sunshine roof

Phantom VI

Improved air conditioning with separate systems for the front and rear compartments, Silver Shadow cylinder heads and Z-bar location for the live rear axle are the main features that distinguish the Phantom VI, introduced in 1968, from the Phantom V. A major departure from standard specification was the special car made for Queen Elizabeth II and having a 6,750cc engine and three-speed GM400 automatic gearbox. Use of the latter made it necessary to fit Shadow-type high-pressure hydraulics whereas production Phantom VIs use the Rolls-Royce-GM four-speed Hydramatic which has provision for the Rolls-Royce mechanical servo.

Engine

Configuration Eight cylinders in vee; light-alloy block and crankcase with wet liners; light-alloy pentroof head with in-line valves operated by push-rods with hydraulic tappets
Dimensions 4.1in × 3.6in (380cu in); 104.4mm × 91.4mm (6,230cc); 6,750cc engine available in 1979
Ignition Single coil with mechanical make and break or Lucas Opus transistorized ignition
Carburation Two SU HD8s
Power output Estimated 200bhp at 4,500rpm

Transmission

Gearbox Rolls-Royce four-step automatic; mechanical servo; GM400 available in 1979

Drive Gearbox in unit with engine; divided propeller shaft
Axle Live; semi-floating; hypoid bevel; ratio 3.89 : 1

Chassis

Type Box section girder with cruciform bracing
Suspension Front: unequal-length wishbones and coil springs; hydraulic dampers; rear: semi-elliptic leaf springs; inboard mounted; remote-control hydraulic shock-absorbers; Z-bar location
Brakes Drum type with Rolls-Royce mechanical servo-assisted hydraulic operation
Wheelbase 144in
Track $60\frac{7}{8}$in (front), 74in (rear)
Weight of chassis 6,010lb
Tyre size 890 × 15

1978 Phantom VI

Corniche

When the Corniche was introduced early in 1971 the company announced that the special-bodied cars would be the engineering and styling leaders for future standard production cars. Built by Mulliner Park Ward, the convertible Corniche is considered to be the ultimate personal Rolls-Royce. The 1971 Corniche was the first of the Shadow series to have the 6,750cc engine and improved air conditioning.

Engine

Configuration Eight cylinders in vee; light-alloy block and crankcase with wet liners; alloy head with in-line valves and pentroof combustion chambers; push-rod valve operation with hydraulic tappets; solid, five main bearing, two-plane crankshaft
Dimensions 4.1in × 3.9in (411.9cu in); 104.4mm × 99mm (6,750cc)
Ignition Single system, initially with mechanical distributor, later with Lucas Opus transistorized operation
Carburation Two SU HD8s fed by SU electric pumps
Power output Approximately 220bhp at 4,500rpm

Transmission

Gearbox General Motors Hydramatic GM400 three-step automatic with torque converter
Drive Gearbox in unit with engine; one-piece propeller shaft
Axle Rubber-mounted, hypoid bevel final-drive unit with universally jointed half shafts; ratio 3.08 : 1
Speeds in gears 1st 50mph; 2nd 83mph; 3rd 120mph

Chassis

Type In unit with body; engine, front suspension and rear suspension carried on two separate subframes
Suspension Front: unequal-length wishbones and coil springs; 1in hydraulic height adjustment; rear: semi-trailing links and coil springs with 3in height adjustment from power hydraulic system
Steering Power-assisted Saginaw re-circulating ball system
Brakes Front and rear, Rolls-Royce-Girling discs; power assistance from 2,000psi hydraulic system; separate hydrostatic rear system
Wheelbase 120in
Track 57½in
Weight of complete car 4,816lb
Tyre size 205 × 15
Performance Standing quarter-mile in 17.1 seconds; 0–50mph in 6.8 seconds; 0–60mph in 9.6 seconds; 0–100mph in 30 seconds

Opposite top: 1978 Corniche saloon
Opposite: 1978 Corniche convertible

Camargue

This latest personal Rolls-Royce was styled by Pininfarina of Turin and first made its appearance in 1975. All the engineering features of the Silver Shadow II are built into the Camargue and it is the first Rolls-Royce to have fully automatic air conditioning. Pininfarina engineered the body to the highest safety standards. Although it has only two doors the model is a full five-seater and is the biggest and heaviest car of the Shadow range.

Engine

Configuration Eight cylinders in vee; light-alloy block and crankcase with wet liners; alloy head with in-line valves and pentroof combustion chambers; push-rod valve operation with hydraulic tappets; solid, five main bearing, two-plane crankshaft
Dimensions 4.1in × 3.9in (411.9cu in); 104.4mm × 99mm (6,750cc)
Ignition Single system; Lucas Opus transistorized operation
Carburation Two SU HD8s fed by SU electric pumps
Power output Approximately 220bhp at 4,500rpm

Transmission

Gearbox General Motors Hydramatic GM400 three-step automatic with torque converter
Drive Gearbox in unit with engine; one-piece propeller shaft
Axle Rubber-mounted, hypoid bevel final-drive unit with universally jointed half shafts; ratio 3.08 : 1
Speeds in gears 1st 47.7mph; 2nd 79.7mph; top 118mph (estimated from maker's figures)

Chassis

Type In unit with body; engine, front and rear suspensions carried on two separate subframes
Suspension Front: unequal-length wishbones and coil springs; 1in of hydraulic height adjustment; rear: semi-trailing links and coil springs with 3in height adjustment from power hydraulic system
Steering Power assisted Saginaw re-circulating ball system
Brakes Front and rear, Rolls-Royce-Girling discs; power assistance from 2,000psi hydraulic system; separate hydrostatic rear system
Wheelbase 120in (short chassis)
Track 57½in
Weight of complete car 5,170lb
Tyre size 235/70 × 15 radial

Opposite top: 1978 Camargue
Opposite: Camargue interior

Silver Shadow II

The adoption of compliant suspension, radial ply, low profile tyres and a lowered compression ratio engine with transistorized ignition, among many other modifications, resulted in a very much improved Silver Shadow, warranting the series II designation. The Silver Shadow II was introduced to the motoring public in 1977. Changes since then have included the addition of an air-dam under the front bumper.

Engine

Configuration Eight cylinders in vee; light-alloy block and crankcase with wet liners; alloy head with in-line valves and pentroof combustion chambers; push-rod valve operation with hydraulic tappets; solid, five main bearing, two-plane crankshaft; compression ratio 8 : 1
Dimensions 4.1in × 3.9in (411.9cu in); 104.4mm × 99mm (6,750cc)
Ignition Single system; Lucas Opus transistorized operation
Carburation Two SU HD8s fed by SU electric pumps
Power output Approximately 220bhp at 4,500rpm

Transmission

Gearbox General Motors Hydramatic GM400 three-step automatic with torque converter
Drive Gearbox in unit with engine; one-piece propeller shaft
Axle Rubber-mounted, hypoid bevel final-drive unit with universally jointed half-shafts; ratio 3.08 : 1
Speeds in gears 1st 56mph; 2nd 94mph; 3rd 116mph

Chassis

Type In unit with body; engine, front and rear suspensions carried on two separate subframes
Suspension Front: unequal-length wishbones and coil springs; 1in of hydraulic height adjustment; built-in compliance; rear: semi-trailing links and coil springs with 3in height adjustment from power hydraulic system
Brakes Front and rear, Rolls-Royce-Girling discs; power assistance from 2,000psi hydraulic system
Wheelbase 120in
Track 57½in
Weight of complete car 4,752lb
Tyre size 235/70 × 15 radial ply
Performance 0–50mph in 7.6 seconds; 0–60mph in 10.6 seconds; 0–100mph in 36.5 seconds

Silver Shadow II of 1979

Silver Wraith II

The Silver Wraith designation was revived in 1977 for the long wheelbase version of the Silver Shadow II.

Engine

Configuration Eight cylinders in vee; light-alloy block and crankcase with wet liners; alloy head with in-line valves and pentroof combustion chambers; push-rod valve operation with hydraulic tappets; solid, five main bearing, two-plane crankshaft; compression ratio 8:1
Dimensions 4.1in × 3.9in (411.9cu in); 104.4mm × 99mm (6,750cc)
Ignition Single system; Lucas Opus transistorized operation
Carburation Two SU HD8s fed by SU electric pumps
Power output Approximately 220bhp at 4,500rpm

Transmission

Gearbox General Motors Hydramatic GM400 three-step automatic with torque converter
Drive Gearbox in unit with engine; one-piece propeller shaft
Axle Rubber-mounted, hypoid bevel final-drive unit with universally jointed half-shafts; ratio 3.08:1
Speeds in gears 1st 56mph; 2nd 94mph; 3rd 116mph

Chassis

Type In unit with body; engine, front and rear suspensions carried on two separate subframes
Suspension Front: unequal-length wishbones and coil springs; 1in of hydraulic height adjustment; built-in compliance; rear: semi-trailing links and coil springs with 3in height adjustment from power hydraulic system
Brakes Front and rear, Rolls-Royce-Girling discs; power assistance from 2,000psi hydraulic system
Wheelbase 124in
Track 57½in
Tyre size 235/70 × 15 radial ply
Performance 0–50mph in 7.6 seconds; 0–60mph in 10.6 seconds; 0–100mph in 36.5 seconds

Opposite: Three views of the Silver Wraith II

ROLLS-ROYCE CLUBS

Founded in 1957, the Rolls-Royce Enthusiasts' Club has a membership of more than 3,500 and is based in Britain. It has 16 sections in the United Kingdom, two in Canada and sections in Austria, Belgium-Holland, France, Hong Kong, Ireland, Switzerland and West Germany. It publishes the RREC *Bulletin* six times a year. The club offers a wide range of services to its members – car insurance, advice on technical matters, historical information, spare parts and specialist advice on such matters as restoration. It plans social gatherings, rallies and commemorative runs at home and abroad, seminars, and visits to museums and factories. It is closely involved with the establishment of the Sir Henry Royce Memorial Foundation. A building has been purchased which will serve both as a permanent home for the club and a repository for archives and memorabilia. Fund raising has begun in order to provide a research library and museum dedicated to the work of Royce and his successors in the company. Membership of the club is open to owners as well as those with a keen interest in Rolls-Royce and Bentley cars although membership at first was restricted to the Rolls-Royce.

The Rolls-Royce Owners' Club is the American-based equivalent of the RREC. It has administrative offices in Mechanicsburg, Pennsylvania, and publishes a club magazine, *The Flying Lady*. Membership exceeds 5,000. Like its British counterpart it organizes rallies and tours, keeps detailed historical records and offers specialist advice on technical matters.

Established in Britain more than 25 years ago, the Twenty Ghost Club has a membership that was at first by invitation only and was restricted to owners of Rolls-Royce cars produced before the Second World War.

The Midland Rolls-Royce Club was established by a group of enthusiasts in the British Midlands. Many of its members also belong to the RREC.

In addition, there are autonomous Rolls-Royce clubs in Australia and South Africa. They hold social gatherings, meets and rallies but often rely on the RREC and the RROC for help on historical and technical matters.

INDEX

Page numbers in italics refer to illustrations. Individual models of Rolls-Royce cars are combined and listed in numerical and alphabetical order under the heading Rolls-Royce models

ACKNOWLEDGMENTS

The compilers of this book wish to thank the following people for their helpfulness and generosity: John Gordon of Frank Dale and Stepsons; Mermie and Ken Karger; John Schroder and the Sir Henry Royce Foundation; the Rolls-Royce Enthusiasts' Club; *Autocar*; the owners who allowed their motor cars to be photographed for this book; and especially Dennis Miller-Williams, David Preston and Cyril Jones of Rolls-Royce Motors.

Copy photography was by Peter Myers. Special photography of cars by Nicky Wright, © Eldorado Books Limited, London, appears on the following pages: 4, 6–7, 38, 52–53, 62–63, 64, 82, 84, 93, 94, 100 (bottom), 102, 103, 104–105, 110–111, 112–113, 116–117, 126–127, 128 (top), 130, 131 (bottom), 132 (bottom), 139, 141.

In the following list of picture credits Rolls-Royce Motors has been abbreviated to RRM and the National Motor Museum, Beaulieu, to NMM. Page 8 Ray Warner (left), W. W. Winter (right); 10 RRM; 11 Peter Roberts; 12 NMM; 13 Mansell Collection; 14–15 NMM; 16 RRM (top); 17 Peter Roberts (top left), RRM (top right); 18–19 NMM; 19 RRM (top left), NMM (top right); 20 RRM; 21 RRM (top), Fox Photos (bottom); 22–26 RRM; 27 RRM (top), LAT Photographic (centre and bottom); 28 W. K. Henderson (top), Peter Roberts (bottom); 29 Doune Motor Museum; 30–31 Thomas Photos, Oxford; 32 NMM; 33 Thomas Photos, Oxford (top and bottom right), *Autocar* (bottom left); 34 *Autocar*; 35 NMM; 36 Royal Automobile Club (top), *Autocar* (bottom); 37 RRM; 39 *Autocar*; 40–41 RRM; 41 *Autocar*; 42–43 Worshipful Company of Coachmakers; 43 RRM; 44 Orbis/Belli (top), Peter Roberts (bottom); 45 RRM; 46 Orbis/Belli; 47 Craven Foundation; 48 NMM (left), *Autocar* (right); 49 Craven Foundation; 50 Peter Roberts; 51 James C. Leake; 54–55 Roger McDonald; 56 RRM; 57 Edward Eves; 58–59 Orbis/ J. Spencer Smith; 60–61 Peter Roberts; 61 Orbis/J. Spencer Smith (top), Orbis/Italfoto (bottom); 62 RRM; 65 Roger Pennington; 66–67 Craven Foundation; 68 Harrah's Automobile Collection (top), M. Karger (bottom); 69–75 M. Karger; 76–77 James C. Leake; 78–81 M. Karger; 85 Nicky Wright; 86–87 Stratford Motor Museum/Orbis/J. Spencer Smith; 87 Dutch National Automobile Museum (top); 88 Peter Roberts; 89 Orbis/J. Spencer Smith; 90–91 Roger Pennington; 92 Peter Roberts; 95 Neill Bruce; 96, 97 Mr Le Comte A. Giansanti-Coluzzi; 98–99 Neill Bruce; 100 Nicky Wright (top); 101 Nicky Wright; 104 *Autocar*; 105 Briggs Cunningham Automotive Museum (top); *Autocar* (bottom); 106 Frank Dale and Stepsons; 107 Mr Le Comte A. Giansanti-Coluzzi, Frank Dale and Stepsons (bottom); 114, 115 Mulliner Park Ward Division RRM; 118 Thomas Photos, Oxford; 119 M. Schumacher; 120 Peter Roberts; 121 RRM; 122, 123 RRM; 124 Daily Telegraph Colour Library/Ivor Lewis; 125 Orbis/J. Spencer Smith; 128 RRM (bottom); 131 RRM (top); 132 RRM (top); 133 RRM; 134 *Autocar*; 135 G. Q. Stiles (top), RRM (bottom); 136 G. Q. Stiles (top); 136–137 RRM; 137 RRM; 138 RRM; 140 Daily Telegraph Colour Library/Ivor Lewis; 142, 143 RRM; 144 Peter Roberts; 146 RRM; 147 Peter Roberts/Science Museum; 149, 151, 153 Peter Roberts; 157, 159 Michael Worthington-Williams; 161 Caffyns (top left and bottom), Michael Worthington-Williams (top right); 163 RRM (top), Caffyns (bottom); 165 NMM (top), Frank Dale and Stepsons (bottom); 167 NMM (top), Frank Dale and Stepsons (bottom); 169 Michael Worthington-Williams; 171 RRM; 173 Mann Egerton (top), Frank Dale and Stepsons (bottom); 175 Michael Worthington-Williams; 177 Frank Dale and Stepsons; 179 Frank Dale and Stepsons (top), RRM (bottom); 181 RRM; 183 Frank Dale and Stepsons (top), RRM (bottom); 185 NMM (top), RRM (bottom); 187 RRM; 189 Frank Dale and Stepsons; 191 RRM (top), Frank Dale and Stepsons (bottom); 193–201 RRM.